TEN-STEP CURRICULUM PLANNING PROCESS MODEL

A CURRICULUM STUDY MAY OR MAY NOT INCLUDE ALL TEN STEPS AND MAY BEGIN OR END WITH ANY ONE STEP IN THE PROCESS

Evaluate Curriculum

Identify Curricular Need

Implement New Curriculum

Develop Curricular Goals and Objectives

Design New Curriculum

Identify Resources and Constraints

Select New Curriculum

Organize Curriculum Committees

Identify New Curricula

Establish Roles of Personnel

WITHDRAWN

CURRICULUM PLANNING: A TEN-STEP PROCESS

by
Weldon F. Zenger, Ed.D.
Fort Hays State University
and
Sharon K. Zenger, Ph.D.
Fort Hays State University

Published by

R & E RESEARCH ASSOCIATES, INC.
Publishers
936 Industrial Avenue
Palo Alto, California 94303

Library of Congress Card Catalog Number
82-60521

I.S.B.N.
0-88247-675-0

cover design by
Valeries Zwinscher

PREFACE

This Handbook was developed as a practical guide for use by school system personnel as they plan and develop curricula. It has also become a very useful instrument to the authors for teaching graduate level curriculum planning and development classes. Much of the information in this Handbook is the result of first hand experiences by the authors as they were working with school systems developing curricula. Because it is a Handbook, not many direct quotes are cited from the literature; however, several references are included for each step of the curriculum planning process as well as a general reference section after the appendixes.

School personnel, especially administrators, are asking for practical, helpful guidelines for studying and planning the curriculum. Theoretical models on the subject seem to be plentiful, but the actual how-to-do-it approaches to curriculum development are much more difficult to locate. This Handbook is designed to serve as a how-to-do-it guide for those who are responsible for organizing and leading school personnel through curriculum studies. It is also designed to be used in college level curriculum planning and development courses. A brief explanation of how it can be used for both is included in the Introduction.

There are many implications that the curriculum planning process in this Handbook has for school systems. They include but are not limited to the following:

- Making the school system accountable.
- Presenting an organized, systematic plan to establish a useful, functional curriculum.
- Giving school officials a basis for curriculum decisions.
- Placing the emphasis of curriculum planning in the hands of the professionals while allowing input from citizens and students.
- Clarifying roles of school personnel and procedures in curriculum development.
- Releasing school officials from the anxiety of worrying about how to plan, study, and develop curricula.
- Furnishing school officials with a clear and concise curriculum planning process which can be used to show how the curriculum was developed.
- Providing a plan of action dealing with any problems centered on or in the school curriculum.

The authors wish to express their gratitude to all the teachers, school administrators, university professors, and graduate students who helped in one way or another with the development of this Handbook. In addition to many Kansas educators contacted, sixty-five university professors and school administrators from throughout central, midwestern, and southeastern parts of the United States were personally interviewed by these writers. All but two or three of those interviewed agreed that the major steps presented in this Handbook are processes and together form a curriculum planning process, although many of them said they had never really thought of these steps as a planning process. All but a couple of those educators interviewed encouraged, some enthusiastically, the writers to develop a systematic process of planning and developing school curricula.

Gratitude is extended to Mrs. Helen Hooper and Mr. Chuck Stones for their continuous advice and assistance. Mrs. Hooper is a Curriculum Coordinator of Unified School District No. 325, Phillipsburg, Kansas; and Mr. Stones is an Assistant Superintendent in charge of Curriculum of Unified School District No. 457, Garden City, Kansas. Also, appreciation is expressed to Dr. Nancy Vogel, Professor of English at Fort Hays State University, who read the manuscript, contributing to the final form.

W.F.Z.
S.K.Z.

TABLE OF CONTENTS

CURRICULUM PLANNING: A TEN-STEP PROCESS

INTRODUCTION

This ten-step curriculum planning process is designed to be used for developing small segments of the school curriculum, adding to the existing program, or creating an entire school curricula. The process brings together parts of the systems approach used more by the business world, and also includes the basic curriculum planning and development processes used by educators. It is a systematic, step-by-step procedure for planning and developing school curricula. The process begins with assessing and stating the curricular need, goes through designing and implementing programs to meet that need, and ends with evaluating the new program to determine to what extent that stated need has been met.

The ten-step process can be used in curriculum planning and development courses preparing college students to lead and guide curricular studies. Administrators and teachers can also use the process to guide district-wide comprehensive curriculum development as well as to design and implement new courses.

How To Use This Handbook

Those using this Handbook probably would acquaint themselves with the entire book by a procedure similar to the one that follows:

1. Read through the ten checklist pages to become familiar with the overall planning process.
2. Thumb through the appendixes to note some of the extra helps provided for planning school curricula.
3. Read through the explanation section for each of the ten steps which explains each step and some suggestions for how to do it.
4. Go through the checklist pages, checking the appropriate spaces for those steps and substeps which are already completed, being done, or not needed. Check the spaces as follows: **CONSIDERING IT**—thinking about doing it but need to study it more; **PLANNING IT**—decided to do it and planning how to do it; **DOING IT**—in the process of carrying out the plan; **COMPLETED**—finished prior to this study or just completed; **NOT NEEDED**—not applicable or not needed for this curriculum study.
5. Go through the checklist pages checking those items and substeps needing more consideration and/or planning as to how to do them.
6. Go through the checklist pages writing and describing on a separate sheet of paper what has

been or is being done for each step and substep in order to accomplish it the way it is marked on the checklist. (See Appendixes D and E for examples of doing this.)

7. Initiate and carry out any curriculum development marked on the checklist as **PLANNING** or **DOING**, and then check the space for **COMPLETED** as the step or substep is finished. Any space checked as **CONSIDERING** should either be changed to **NOT NEEDED** or **COMPLETED**, whichever is the case.

These ten steps are not necessarily in the order that they will be used to develop curricula. Also, all steps will not necessarily be used for every curriculum study. The users should utilize those steps and substeps that are needed, in the order they are needed, to fit their unique situations to solve their particular curricular problems. They can do this by first going through all ten steps and substeps, checking those on the checklist that are already completed or not needed for their study. Planners may find it necessary to use steps and substeps later in the development process that they did not plan to use at first. They should be careful not to become bogged down with how to do one step before going through all of them. One long step could make the entire process seem more difficult than it really is, resulting in unnecessary delay and frustration.

The checklist should be marked with a lead pencil so the marks can be erased. Those using the checklist may find that they want to change their responses and being able to erase them will help to keep the checklist from becoming messy and confusing. Also, the checklist can be used over again when the marks have been erased. An explanation of what has been done or is being planned to do for each item checked should be written on separate paper. (See the two simulated studies, Appendixes D and E, for examples as to how the checklist can be used.)

Use in College/University Curriculum Classes

The ten-step process is designed to be used in college curriculum planning and development courses to assist in planning how to solve real or simulated curricular problems. These writers, when teaching courses, require that class participants identify a curricular problem or need at the beginning of each course. Next, the steps and substeps of the ten-step process are thoroughly studied and discussed. The participants then individually, or in small groups, follow the ten-step process to develop a plan for solving their curricular problem. They do not solve the problem, but they do develop a course of action for solving it. As a final part of their curriculum planning assignment, the students orally present their plans to the class. They have to defend and justify their plans for solving the curricular problems to the other class members. This procedure enables class participants to learn how the ten-step process can be used to solve various kinds of curricular problems.

Use by School Practitioners

The ten-step process is designed to be used by administrators as a guide for leading the faculty through comprehensive curriculum studies. By checking off the steps and substeps as they are completed, administrators can determine the exact progress of a study at all times. Also by following the checklist, teachers and administrators can use this curriculum planning process as a guide to study, design, implement, and evaluate a new program, subject, topic, or course, and know exactly what is happening at any given time.

STEP I

STATE THE CURRICULUM PROBLEM OR NEED—

CONDUCT A NEEDS ASSESSMENT IF NECESSARY

STATING THE CURRICULUM PROBLEM OR NEED IS USUALLY THE FIRST STEP IN ANY TYPE OF CURRICULUM STUDY. IF THE NEED IS OBVIOUS AND CAN BE STATED IN WRITING AND AGREED UPON BY THOSE INVOLVED, THIS STEP CAN BE OMITTED. HOWEVER, IF THERE IS A PROBLEM BUT THE NEED TO SOLVE THAT PROBLEM IS NOT CLEAR OR THE NEED SHOULD BE VERIFIED, AN ASSESSMENT SHOULD BE CONDUCTED TO CLARIFY THE NEED. BY READING THROUGH STEP I, THE CURRICULUM PLANNER SHOULD BE ABLE TO DETERMINE IF A NEEDS ASSESSMENT IS NECESSARY.

	CONSIDERING IT	PLANNING IT	DOING IT	COMPLETED	NOT NEEDED
I. STATE THE CURRICULUM PROBLEM OR NEED—CONDUCT A NEEDS ASSESSMENT IF NECESSARY.					
A. IDENTIFY PROBLEM OR NEED					
1. IF KNOWN, STATE THE CURRICULUM PROBLEM OR NEED					
2. IF THE NEED IS UNKNOWN OR SHOULD BE VERIFIED, CONDUCT NEEDS ASSESSMENT					
a. DETERMINE WHAT IS PRESENTLY BEING DONE (WHAT NOW EXISTS), IF ANYTHING					
b. DETERMINE WHAT IS WANTED OR INTENDED					
c. SELECT OR DEVELOP DATA GATHERING INSTRUMENT (QUESTIONNAIRE, INTERVIEW GUIDE, ETC.)					
d. COLLECT AND ORGANIZE INFORMATION					
e. ANALYZE DATA; COMPARE WHAT IS WANTED WITH WHAT ACTUALLY IS IN THE CURRICULUM. THE DIFFERENCE IS THE CURRICULAR NEED.					
B. QUICK ASSESSMENT AND COORDINATION OF THE CURRICULUM—IF AN EXTENSIVE NEEDS ASSESSMENT IS NOT DESIRED, OR AFTER A NEEDS ASSESSMENT IS COMPLETED					

STEP I: EXPLANATION SECTION

I. STATE THE PROBLEM OR NEED—CONDUCT A NEEDS ASSESSMENT IF NECESSARY

A. IDENTIFY NEED OR PROBLEM

1. IF KNOWN, STATE THE CURRICULUM PROBLEM OR NEED

The first step in any curriculum study usually is to state the problem or need in writing. There has to be a reason for doing the study: someone must think something is not working properly, wants to make sure what is being done is correct, or wants to look for possible improvements or total new concepts. Adding to or changing the curriculum simply for the sake of change is inexcusable. Before attempting to decide if an innovation or new program should become a part of the curriculum, it should be determined if the innovation will in some way contribute to or fulfill a need or goal of the school system. It may be that the problem can be diagnosed informally at this point; that is, an attempt made to determine informally whatever is wanted as well as what now exists (current status).

It is possible that what is wanted, and that it does not presently exist, is easily recognized. If this is the case, the need is obvious and a formal needs assessment is not necessary. If so, the need should be stated as clearly as possible in writing and plans made to proceed to Step II of this planning process. This informal assessment may be done by having the teachers write out in detail what they want (objectives) and what is actually happening at the present time, thus pointing out the difference which is the curricular need.

2. IF THE NEED IS UNKNOWN OR SHOULD BE VERIFIED, CONDUCT A NEEDS ASSESSMENT

If the curriculum need or problem cannot be clearly defined or if this need requires validation, then a needs assessment should be conducted. The first step in conducting a needs assessment is to place someone in charge who has both *authority* and *responsibility*. This individual may form a committee to assist or advise; however, the main assistance required is usually secretarial help. It is common for administrators to conduct the needs assessment themselves. If more assistance regarding how to conduct a needs assessment is desired than is offered in this Handbook, local universities and state departments of education are sources which can be contacted.

a. DETERMINE WHAT IS PRESENTLY BEING DONE (WHAT NOW EXISTS) IF ANYTHING

If it is clear nothing exists in the present curriculum that is wanted, this Substep should be omitted, and the results of (Substeps b and/or d) should be considered as the curricular need. If, however, there are things going on in the present curriculum which apply to what is wanted, and there usually are, then those things must be clarified and subtracted from what is stated as wanted in (Substeps b and/or d). This difference or gap is the need.

One way to clarify what now exists in a school curriculum is to conduct an inventory of the present programs or subject areas. This can be done by examining current curriculum guides. If guides are not available, the teachers from each program or subject area (or whatever is being studied), can list what they are presently doing in each course. This can be in the form of:

- Main concepts, topics, knowledge, skills.
- Goals or general objectives.
- Course content—scope and sequence, for each course.

If what exists in the curriculum is not clearly defined on paper, which it may not be, it may be easier to identify and delineate content or objectives at the course level first; maybe even at the unit, chapter, mod, or lesson level; then bring them together to form the general content or goals for each subject area.

If it becomes necessary to determine how well "what now exists" is being achieved, the following data can be consulted:

- Test results.
- Student grades.
- Performance records.
- Teacher records and comments.
- Student follow-up questionnaires.
- Past curricula evaluations.

b. DETERMINE WHAT IS WANTED OR INTENDED

That which is wanted or intended in the curriculum may already be stated in the form of goals or objectives. Goals state what is wanted (the intent) for the entire curriculum, program, or subject areas; objectives do the same for subjects, courses, or classes. If what is wanted is known in the form of goals or in some other manner, the planner should proceed to (Substep e) of this Step I and determine the need.

If no goals or objectives exist or any other information stating what is wanted, it will be necessary to begin by determining the needs and desires of whoever and whatever is affected. A question which seems to arise when seeking this information is, "Who should be queried?" There is, of course, no pat answer to this question. If the patrons are to be involved and it is a small school, all parents, faculty, and school board members should be included. Then, other members of the community can be informed as to what is being done through the news media and a request can be issued that they contact the school if interested in participating. For larger systems, some type of random sample may be necessary. It might be best to seek the advice of research specialists to determine the sampling procedure to be used. The following should be considered when seeking information about what is wanted in the curriculum:

- Community.
- Staff.
- Parents.
- Students and former students.
- College—requirements.
- State—requirements.
- National requirements.

- Other _____.

c. SELECT OR DEVELOP DATA GATHERING INSTRUMENT (QUESTION-NAIRE, INTERVIEW GUIDE, ETC.)

To determine what is wanted or intended in a curriculum or program, information has to be collected. This usually requires a data-gathering instrument or device of some type. That information is often gathered through a survey of some type, frequently a questionnaire. Some instruments and sources which can be used to acquire information are:

- Questionnaires.
- Interviews—personal, groups, clubs.
- Checklists.
- Rating scales.
- Tests and inventories.
- Grades.
- Observations.
- Records—personal, school, community.
- Other _____.

The actual instruments or devices for gathering the necessary information may be selected, if there are any available; or they may have to be developed. More than likely, the instrument will have to be developed, and the budget may determine the type of device that is constructed. It can be any type of technique or instrument that extracts the needed information from the source. In the construction of a needs assessment instrument, the type of information required will first have to be identified, and then, statements or questions that will yield that information developed. One way to develop these statements is by having those individuals or a sampling of those who are involved or affected by the curriculum study, submit statements about what they think is needed or required to meet that particular need. Statements can also be based on information from the literature or statements from other needs assessment instruments. These statements can be compared and consolidated; and duplications can be eliminated. The statements then can be rewritten into the questions or statements necessary to gain the information required to determine whether or not there is a curriculum need.

The needs assessment instrument should have a place where those being queried can respond to each statement. This response can be in the form of a *yes* or *no*, selection from several choices, a space checked on a continuum, or in any number of ways to indicate preferences. Those who are developing the instrument should determine how the collected information will be used and who will have access to it.

One of the most used instruments for conducting a needs assessment is the questionnaire. However, questionnaires as well as other needs assessment instruments are so varied, and specialized for each situation, that no attempt is made here to show examples. To begin to locate available instruments or for assistance in developing them, the following should be contacted:

- Local colleges and universities.

- Large educational publishing companies.
- Educational and professional associations.
- State and national departments of education.

d.   COLLECT AND ORGANIZE INFORMATION

At this point the questionnaire should be sent out, and the interviews or observations conducted to gather the information required to determine what is wanted or intended in the curriculum. As much information as possible should be collected. Several follow-up letters, phone calls, and personal contacts are good ways of getting information that is not acquired initially. If the data is already available through tests or other files and records, then the survey, questionnaire, and interviews are not necessary. Whatever the technique, it is advisable to gather as much data as possible or needed, and organize it into some type of form or system so that it can be analyzed. The information could be developed into goal statements at this point, if desired. However, constructing goal statements may take too much time and sidetrack the needs assessment process. The information collected will be what is wanted, whether or not it is stated in the form of goals. (See Step II to develop goals.) It must be in some type of written form, however, so it can be used to determine the curricular need.

e.   ANALYZE DATA; COMPARE WHAT IS WANTED WITH WHAT NOW AC-TUALLY EXISTS IN THE CURRICULUM. THE DIFFERENCE IS THE CUR-RICULAR NEED.

Now that what actually exists in the curriculum (Substep a) and that which is wanted (Substeps b and/or d) have been established, the difference can be determined by using a matrix. In the horizontal columns of the matrix, the planner should list "what is wanted." If goal statements have been developed, they should be used. If not, the information should be listed in some type of written form. In the vertical columns, "what now exists" should be listed. This can be done in the form of main concepts, topics, goals, or content of the program, subject areas, or the courses within a subject area. It should be noted that a square is formed where the "what is wanted" and "what exists" columns intersect. If the "what is wanted" is already being done by "what exists," a check mark should be made in the square where the two columns meet. If the "what is wanted" is not being done or being done suffi-ciently, that square should be left blank. After the matrix is completed, the blank squares will show those items that are wanted but are not being accomplished by the present curri-cula, thus the curricular need.

The matrix that follows illustrates how this process works; district-wide goals are listed in the horizontal columns and Business Education goals are listed in the vertical columns. Then, an X is placed in the square where the two goals intersect. If the Business Education goal fulfills or contributes in some way to the district goals, an X is marked in the proper box. This matrix shows which district goals Business Education is helping to accomplish. By marking the chart for all subject areas within the curriculum, it can be determined how many subject area goals throughout the curriculum are contributing to each district goal. This visual

NEEDS ASSESSMENT MATRIX

List what already exists in these columns--subject area/course goals, or main topics.

BUSINESS EDUCATION GOALS

List what is wanted in these columns--goal statements or any written statements indicating what is wanted in the curriculum.

USD #000 EDUCATIONAL GOALS	1. Develop skills to become employable in the business environment as well as for personal use.	2. Learn to become intelligent consumers of the services of business.	3. Form a clear understanding of the nation's economy.	4. Develop respect for the rights and thoughts of other individuals.	5. Realize career opportunities available to them.	6.	7.	8.
1. Develop skills in reading, writing, speaking and listening.	X							
2. Acquire mathematical skills.		X						
3. Comprehend and practice democratic ideas and ideals.				X				
4. Gain knowledge about how to be a good citizen.				X				
5. Acquire skills to enter a specific field of work.	X				X			
6. Learn how to be a good manager of money, property, and resources.		X						
7. Practice and understand the ideas of health and safety.								
8. Form good character, self-worth, respect, and pride.				X				
9. Learn to respect and get along with people with whom we work and live.				X				
10. Understand and practice the skills of family living.				X				
11. Develop a desire for learning now and in the future.	X				X			
12. Comprehend how to examine and use information.	X	X						
13. Gain knowledge about how to respect and get along with people who think, dress, and act differently.				X				
14. Learn how to use leisure time.	X							
15. Attempt to understand the changes that take place in the world.			X					
16. Appreciate culture and beauty in the world.								
17.								
18.								

summary points out any district goals that are being over- or under-emphasized, as well as things that may be happening in the curriculum for which there are no goals. Graphically, this charting process shows the difference between what is wanted in the curriculum and what is actually happening, the curricular need.

The matrix shows the difference between "what is wanted" and "what exists" in the curriculum, and this is the curricular need. This same process, using a matrix, can be used for the entire school district's curriculum, a program, a subject area (discipline) within the curriculum, or even one course within a subject area. By placing "what is wanted" in one column and "what exists" in the other, the difference or need can be determined and easily seen.

Curricular needs assessment is a continuous process, however. Since society changes, people change, and circumstances in general may change; consequently, the needs of a school system may vary from year to year.

B. **QUICK ASSESSMENT AND COORDINATION OF THE CURRICULUM—IF AN EXTENSIVE NEEDS ASSESSMENT IS NOT DESIRED, OR AFTER A NEEDS ASSESSMENT IS COMPLETED.**

If there is no particular curriculum need or problem but an overall picture of what is happening is desired, the following assessment process can be used. This process provides for the coordination of content scope and sequence of the curriculum K-12 as well as for programs and subject areas within the curriculum. If (Substep B2) is completed, the process also provides for somewhat of an evaluation of the curriculum. *Note:* Read through the remaining part of this Substep before deciding whether or not to do it.

1. Each teacher should identify the major areas of knowledge, concepts, topics, content, or skills covered for each grade level he/she teaches.

2. Each teacher compares these major topics with other sources such as various textbooks, professional literature, other school systems, and the National Typical Course of Study (1978). He/she may make changes if desired.

3. Each teacher indicates on a matrix (using an agreed-upon key) to what extent each topic is being taught in his/her class.

4. Kindergarten and first grade teachers meet to determine where kindergarten content will leave off and where first grade content will begin in each subject area. Some overlap, even total overlap, may be wanted and even necessary in some cases. This procedure will prevent unwanted overlap and duplication as well as omission of curriculum content.

5. First grade teachers and second grade teachers meet to do the same as the kindergarten and first grade teachers did. Then the second grade teachers and the third grade teachers meet and so on up through all grade levels. *A principal or curriculum coordinator should always be present at these meetings to help resolve differences.*

The following example illustrates how a matrix can be used to coordinate the curriculum content. This example shows how K-5 teachers in one school completed the matrix

SUBJECT OF CURRICULUM AREA – SOCIAL STUDIES

I - INTRODUCED--FORMALLY PRESENTED FOR THE FIRST TIME

KEY: D - DEVELOPED--STRESSED THOROUGHLY

R - REVIEWED--REVIEWED, REINFORCED OR STRESSED LIGHTLY AGAIN

CONTENT/CRITICAL SKILLS/TOPICS	K	1	2	3	4	5	6	7	8	9	10	11	12
Interpreting map symbols, scales, legends, and keys				I	D	R							
Using the grid system on maps and globes				I	D	D							
Making and interpreting charts and graphs					I	D							
Reading and using time lines					I	D							
Vocabulary building	I	D	D	D	D	D							
Picture interpretation				I	D	R							
Distinguishing fact, opinion, attitude, and judgment					I	D							
Outlining				I	D	R							
Note taking					I	D							
Making oral and written reports				I	D	R							
Recognizing cause and effect					I	D							
Interpreting source material					I	D							
Interpreting political cartoons						I							
Using reference materials				I	D	D							
Developing chronological concepts					I	D							
Comprehension	I	D	D	D	D	D							
Organizing information				I	D	R							
Interpreting graphics					I	D							
Problem Solving				I	D	R							
Observing	I	D	R	R	R	R							
Defining		I	D	R	R	R							
Generalizing					I	D							
Synthesizing					I	D							
Predicting		I	D	R	R	R							
Evaluating					I	D	R						
Effective Listening	I	D	D	R	R	R							
Learning to use:													
1. Table of content			I	D	R	R							
2. Index				I	D	R							
3. Newspapers					I	D							
4. Dictionaries				I	D	D							
5. Encyclopedias				I	D	D							
6. Glossary				I	D	R							
7. Library				I	D	D							
Reading and making simple charts				I	D	D							
Thinking and inquiry			I	D	R	R							
Planning and organizing				I	D	D							
Doing research and investigation					I	D							
Reading diagrams				I	D	R							
Identification		I	D	R	R	R							
Recall			I	D	D	R							
Differentiation		I	D	D	R	R							
Inferring					I	D							
Comparing	I	D	D	R	R	R							
Classifying				I	D	D							
Hypothesizing					I	D							
Using the calendar	I	D	D	R	R	R							

for their social studies program. The matrix shows what, when, and in how much depth the content is taught in grades kindergarten through five.

The teachers in this example did not take time to do (Substep B2) of the quick assessment. Therefore, this is an example of solely coordinating the content in the present curriculum. In addition to coordinating curriculum, the process can be used as a curriculum assessment or even curriculum evaluation. By doing what is called for in (Substep B2), that is, comparing the content in the present curriculum with that used and recommended by other curricular sources, judgments can be made about adding or deleting content to the curriculum. Making judgments involves making evaluations; and when judgments about curriculum content are made, it becomes curriculum evaluation.

If the social studies teachers used in this example would do (Substep B2) of the quick assessment, it is possible that they would include somewhat more social studies content and activities in the kindergarten, first, and second grades. (Substep B2) does take a considerable amount of time, however, and it is often not done at first and sometimes not at all. If teachers do decide to do (Substep B2), they usually prefer to do it before they coordinate their present curriculum. It is double work to coordinate the curriculum and then have to coordinate it again after the content has been changed. This is the reason (Substep B2) is included early in the Step and not after (Substep B5) of the quick assessment. By placing it where it is, teachers can make decisions about whether or not to compare what they have in their curriculum with other curricula before they coordinate it throughout all grade levels.

The matrix indicates if anything is being repeated more than is necessary, as well as revealing if anything is not being emphasized enough or maybe even omitted completely. It gives a quick overview of what is and what is not being done. It can also show coordination of the curriculum K-12 both vertically and horizontally through the school system.

REFERENCES

Ainsworth, C.S. "Curricular Aims and the Analysis of Needs Statements." *British Journal of Educational Studies,* October, 1976, *24*, 219-232.

Budnik, Thomas J. "An Estimate of the Reliability of a Technique of Increasing Educational Accountability through Goal Analysis Involving Community, Staff, and Students." *The Journal of Educational Research*, May/June, 1978, *71*, 251-256.

Clegg, Ambrose A., Jr. "The Teacher as Manager of the Curriculum?" *Educational Leadership*, January, 1973, *30*, 307-309.

Doll, Ronald C. *Curriculum Improvement* (4th ed.). Boston: Allyn and Bacon, 1978.

English, Fenwick W. and Kaufman, Roger A. *Needs Assessment: A focus for Curriculum Development*.

Washington, D.C.: Association for Supervision and Curriculum Development, 1975.

Fine, Thomas W. "Implementing a Needs Assessment Program." *Educational Technology*, February, 1980, *20*, 30-31.

Gottesman, Alexander M. "Applying a Model in Curriculum Planning." *NASSP Bulletin*, October, 1977, *61*, 24-30.

Griffith, William S. "Educational Needs: Definitions, Assessment, and Utilization." *School Review*, May, 1978, *86*, 382-393.

Hays, Donald G. "Needs Assessment: A Counseling Prerequisite." *NASSP Bulletin*, September, 1977, *19*, 11-16.

Kaufman, Roger and English, Fenwick W. *Needs Assessment*. Englewood Cliffs, NJ: Educational Technology Publications, 1979.

Marshall, John F. and Sorochty, Roger W. "Assessing the Need to Reorganize: A Process Model." *NASPA Journal*, February, 1976, 13-16.

Mosrie, David. "Assessing School Needs: A Practical Approach." *NASSP Bulletin*, November, 1980, *64*, 64-67.

Nault, William H. *Typical Course of Study*. Chicago: Field Enterprises Educational Corp., 1978.

Neagley, Ross L. and Evans, N. Dean. *Handbook for Effective Curriculum Development*. Englewood Cliffs, NJ: Prentice-Hall, 1967.

Patterson, Jerry L. and Czajkowski, Theodore J. "District Needs Assessment: One Avenue to Program Improvement." *Phi Delta Kappan*, December, 1976, *58*, 327-329.

Peterson, Betty (Ed.). *Staff Development/Organization Development*. Alexandria, VA: Association for Supervision and Curriculum Development, 1981.

Pratt, David. *Curriculum, Design and Development*. New York: Harcourt Brace Jovanovich, 1980.

Saylor, Galen J.; Alexander, William M.; and Lewis, Arthur J. *Curriculum Planning for Better Teaching and Learning* (4th ed.). Chicago: Holt, Rinehart and Winston, 1981.

Stiltner, Barbara. "Needs Assessment: A First Step." *Elementary School Guidance and Counseling*, April, 1978, *12*, 239-246.

Tankard, George C., Jr. *Curriculum Improvement: An Administrator's Guide*. West Nyack, NY: Parker, 1974.

Tyler, Ralph W. "Specific Approaches to Curriculum Development." In James R. Gress and David E. Purpel (Eds.), *Curriculum, An Introduction to the Field*. Berkeley: McCutchan, 1978.

Wiles, Jon and Bondi, Joseph, Jr. *Curriculum Development*. Columbus: Charles E. Merrill, 1979.

Williams, William H. "Major Steps in Developing Curriculum." *Industrial Education*, September, 1971, *60*, 79-81.

Zenger, Weldon F. "A System for Showing Curriculum Accountability Through Curriculum Development and Evaluation." Hays, KS: Copyright, 1973.

IDENTIFY, REVISE, OR DEVELOP CURRICULUM/PROGRAM GOALS AND OBJECTIVES

Step II will describe goals and objectives, as well as their use and development. This does not necessarily mean that they have to be developed only at this point when developing curricula. Goals and objectives are placed as Step II because they are so intertwined with Step I, Stating the Need.

Note: The planner should refer back to Step II as needed while going through the other steps of this process of developing curricula.

If goals have been developed either in Step I or previously, the first part (goals) of this Step will not be needed. The second part (developing objectives) will be needed more in some of the later steps of this process. Therefore, Step II may not be used at this stage but referred back to as needed.

If goals or objectives are to be developed at this point, planners should consider Steps III, IV, and V first. These three steps serve as a guide for planning and organizing curriculum studies. Since writing goals and objectives is a curriculum study in and of itself, it may be necessary to plan and organize for that study first. If goals are developed as the first step and the needs have not been determined, curriculum planners should then go back to Step I to determine if a needs assessment is necessary before going on with the study.

GOALS AND OBJECTIVES EXPLAINED

Goals and objectives can be defined and used in many ways. In this Handbook, goals are described as broad general statements of intent while objectives are statements of specific expected outcomes of the learner. Program goals (general objectives) are used when dealing with programs or subject areas (disciplines) within the curriculum. They are written the same as the school district goals except they are for a particular program or subject area. Two types of objectives are used in the Handbook. Terminal objectives for courses are relatively specific statements of major learning outcomes, and student behavioral objectives are statements of very specific outcomes of instruction.

Each of these goals and objectives is described more in the following pages. In addition, guidelines for writing them as well as examples are included. Since a school philosophy precedes the development of goals and objectives, a description and example of it is also presented.

STEP II

		CONSIDERING IT	PLANNING IT	DOING IT	COMPLETED	NOT NEEDED
II.	IDENTIFY, REVISE, OR DEVELOP SCHOOL CURRICULUM/PROGRAM GOALS AND OBJECTIVES					
A.	IDENTIFY, REVISE, OR DEVELOP SCHOOL DISTRICT PHILOSOPHY					
B.	IDENTIFY, REVISE, OR DEVELOP SCHOOL DISTRICT (SYSTEM-WIDE) GOALS					
C.	IDENTIFY, REVISE, OR DEVELOP GOALS (GENERAL OBJECTIVES) OF PROGRAMS OR SUBJECT AREAS (DISCIPLINES) OF THE SCHOOL CURRICULUM					
D.	IDENTIFY, REVISE, OR DEVELOP COURSE TERMINAL OBJECTIVES OF THE SCHOOL COURSES					
E.	IDENTIFY, REVISE, OR DEVELOP STUDENT BEHAVIORAL OBJECTIVES OF THE SCHOOL COURSES					

STEP II: EXPLANATION SECTION

II. **IDENTIFY, REVISE, OR DEVELOP SCHOOL CURRICULUM/PROGRAM GOALS AND OBJECTIVES**

A. **IDENTIFY, REVISE, OR DEVELOP SCHOOL DISTRICT PHILOSOPHY**

A school district philosophy is a very general statement, encompassing purpose, intent, and direction. It reflects the values and beliefs of a school district, its beliefs about the individual. The school philosophy is used as a guide for developing school goals.

Here is an example of a school philosophy:

Unified School District No. 000 will provide an educational environment that recognizes the individual differences of all students; that encourages each individual to develop to his/her highest possible potential mentally, physically, and socially; that promotes a positive self-image, self-discipline, self-respect, respect for others and others' property, a sense of patriotism, and respect for authority. The district will also provide a broad curriculum that enables individuals to think creatively, critically, and constructively; to recognize and solve problems logically; and to function as effective and responsible citizens of a democratic society.

B. **IDENTIFY, REVISE OR DEVELOP SCHOOL DISTRICT (SYSTEM-WIDE) GOALS**
STATEMENT OF GOALS

Goals are broad, general statements of intent. They are general statements of intended outcomes, of what is wanted, desired, or intended. They usually are not written in measurable terms and are few in number.

Goals can be written from either the teacher's or learner's point of view.

Examples of goals:

Develop good study habits (this could be from either the teacher's or student's point of view).

Learn how to use good study habits (more from the student's point of view).

Provide for the learning of good study habits (from the teacher's point of view).

One way to make certain goals are clear is to state that the learner, student, or participant is to do it.

Example: The learner is to develop good study habits.

Example of system-wide goals:

One of the best examples of school system goals is the Education Goal Statements (1972) developed by the California School Board Association and distributed by the Phi Delta Kappa. These goal statements with a brief introduction follow:

EDUCATIONAL GOALS

The 18 goals used in this program were derived from the 18 goal categories developed in 1969 by the California School Board Association. This list was completed after a thorough analysis of goals from other states, pilot schools of California's Planning, Program, Budgeting System and other sources. The research indicated that the 18 goal categories of the California School Board Association were all encompassing and acceptable as a starting point for most citizens of the community. From the many field tests which have been conducted using these 18 goals, it has been found community members rarely suggest additional goals and the 18 goals are accepted as legitimate aims of educational institutions.

GOALS:

- Learn how to be a good citizen.
- Learn how to respect and get along with people who think, dress and act differently.
- Learn about and try to understand the changes that take place in the world.
- Develop skills in reading, writing, speaking, and listening.
- Understand and practice democratic ideas and ideals.
- Learn how to examine and use information.
- Understand and practice the skills of family living.
- Learn to respect and get along with people with whom we work and live.
- Develop skills to enter a specific field of work.
- Learn how to be a good manager of money, property, and resources.
- Develop a desire for learning now and in the future.
- Learn how to use leisure time.
- Practice and understand the ideas of health and safety.
- Appreciate culture and beauty in the world.
- Gain information needed to make job selections.
- Develop pride in work and a feeling of self-worth.
- Develop good character and self-respect.
- Develop skills in mathematics and science. *(Phi Delta Kappa, 1978)*

DEVELOPMENT OF DISTRICT GOALS

School district goals are broad, general statements of directions, purpose, and intent of the school system. They are statements of what is wanted or intended in general terms. They are more specific than the school district philosophy but not so specific as course objectives.

To develop system-wide goals (what's wanted or intended), the same procedure should be followed as when doing a needs assessment. That is, determine the needs and desires of whoever is concerned. In most cases, this will involve some or all of the following:

- Community.
- Staff.

- Parents.
- Former Students.
- College—requirements.
- State—requirements.
- National needs.

Some methods of collecting information include:
- Questionnaires.
- Surveys.
- Meetings of various groups—including community and civic groups.
- Interviews.
- Records—school and community.
- Tests and inventories.

With information from these sources, curriculum (system or district-wide) goals can be written. The goals or goal statements are actually summary statements of what was stated as needs or desires by those who are involved. It is also possible to develop a statement of school philosophy from this same information. Because a statement of philosophy is even more general than goals, it should precede the establishment of curriculum goals. Goal statements must not only be broad and general, but flexible enough to state the needs and values of a school system and give direction to curriculum planning and development as well.

ONE METHOD OF DEVELOPING DISTRICT-WIDE GOALS

One way to develop school system-wide (district) curriculum goals is to survey the community using a questionnaire and modified version of the Delphi Technique. The Delphi Technique is a method of surveying a group to reach consensus or near consensus without bringing the group together. A questionnaire is composed of goal statements such as the Phi Delta Kappa Educational Goal Statements (1978). It is sent out to members of the community two or three times to establish and prioritize the goal statements. The responses to the survey such as a questionnaire of goal statements are compiled, showing and explaining the results, and then returned to those responding to see if they want to change their responses after seeing how others replied. Those respondents who are not in agreement with the majority are encouraged to change their responses or state the reason for their different beliefs from the majority. The main advantage of the Delphi Technique is that it is anonymous, which means influential individuals and persuasive talkers have no more influence on the group than anyone else. According to Hostrop (1973), House (1973), and Hartman (1981), respondents who have views different from those of the majority will tend to change to the same as the majority, and therefore, establish a consensus or near consensus of a group which is another advantage of the Delphi Technique.

Each school district should revise these California School Board Statements to suit its particular system.(The writers have found that some districts reword and consolidate some of the statements. Districts have frequently added a goal statement pertaining specifically to mathematics. Also, some systems have not included the statement, "Gain a general education," because it is so broadly stated that everything in the curriculum fits into it.) The writers have found the statement made in the paragraph preceding these goals to be very true. That is, they are acceptable as a starting point for most citizens of the community; community members rarely suggest additional goals to them; and they are accepted as legitimate aims of educational institutions.

The first questionnaire should list the existing goals of the district, those developed by the California School Board Association, a combination of the two or others of some kind. The patrons are then encouraged to add any goals they think should be a part of the district's curriculum. Those who are in charge of the survey incorporate goals suggested by the patrons, with those listed on the first questionnaire and send them out as a second questionnaire asking the patrons to rate them as to importance on a scale of 1-5, 1-10, or any scale that can be averaged mathematically. The numerical responses to the second questionnaire are figured mathematically and ranked. These goal statements are then listed according to ranked priority of the patrons. Next, this list of prioritized goals is sent to those patrons responding to the survey and then used as a basis for updating the goals of the school district. The first questionnaire should be accompanied by a letter from the district superintendent or board of education explaining what is being done and the procedure for doing it. A sample letter follows:

UNIFIED SCHOOL DISTRICT NO. 000

April 13, 1982

Dear Patron:

The educational goals for Unified School District No. 000 are being reviewed and updated this year. To assure that these goals reflect the wishes of the community, school patrons are being asked to help. Your participation in this endeavor will certainly be appreciated.

A questionnaire is being used to seek information about what you think the purposes and goals of U.S.D. No. 000 should be. The questionnaire will be used in the following manner.

1. The first questionnaire will include some of the educational goals that are considered as acceptable for educational institutions. You are asked to consider them, cross out, or add goals as you think they should be. (This is what you think the school system should be doing not what you think it is doing.)

2. The second questionnaire will include those goals that were not eliminated as well as those that were added to the first questionnaire. It will be sent to those patrons who responded to the first questionnaire asking them to rate the importance of each goal for U.S.D. No. 000.

3. Each patron who responded to the second questionnaire will receive a copy of the survey's final results. This information will then be used as basis for updating the goals of U.S.D. No. 000.

The first questionnaire and a self-addressed, stamped envelope are enclosed with this letter. Would you please give it serious consideration and return it at your earliest convenience?

Sincerely,

John Doe
Superintendent

C. IDENTIFY, REVISE, OR DEVELOP GOALS (GENERAL OBJECTIVES) OF PROGRAMS OR SUBJECT AREAS (DISCIPLINES) OF THE SCHOOL CURRICULUM

Goals or general objectives used for programs or subject areas (mathematics, science, reading, etc.) within the curriculum are written almost the same as system-wide goals except they are for a particular program or subject area. Since a particular program or subject area is not as encompassing as the entire curriculum, these goals usually are not quite so broad and general as district-wide goals.

Examples of goals for a reading program:

The learner is:

To gain a basic understanding of the purpose and function of reading.

To develop adequate knowledge and skills required to be an effective reader.

To acquire reading skills necessary for adapting to a changing computerized society.

To establish a broad and sufficient vocabulary for reading at appropriate levels.

DEVELOPMENT OF PROGRAM/SUBJECT AREA GOALS

The terms "goals" and "general objectives" are often used interchangeably when referring to programs or subject areas within the curriculum. They can be developed by having teachers write out the major areas of knowledge, concepts, topics, and skills they cover in their subjects and/or grades for each year. The teachers then should consult other sources for that same information. Other sources can include textbooks on the subject, professional and educational literature, curriculum guides of other school systems, as well as state and national curriculum guides. One good national source is the *Typical Course of Study* published by Field Enterprises Educational Corporation (1978). Once what is being taught, or is going to be taught, is identified, teachers can write general statements such as those previously stated for the reading program. These general statements are the goals or general objectives of the subject area or program.

D. IDENTIFY, REVISE, OR DEVELOP COURSE TERMINAL OBJECTIVES OF THE SCHOOL COURSES

STATEMENTS OF OBJECTIVES

Objectives are statements of specific expected outcomes of what the learner is to be like or be able to do when the objective has been achieved. Objectives are used as a means to fulfill and accomplish goals. They are stated in measurable terms so it can be determined when they have or have not been achieved and are written from the learner's point of view.

COURSE TERMINAL OBJECTIVES

Terminal behavioral objectives are relatively specific statements of the major learning outcomes. They are stated in broad terms, yet specific enough to identify what the learner is to be able to do at the end of the course. A course terminal objective may be a summary statement of the behavioral objectives for a set amount of instruction such as units or chapters. However, any broad statement that specifies what the learner is able to do at the end of a course can be classified as a course terminal objective.

Examples:

Course Terminal Objectives

At the end of this unit, the student should be able to state how energy interacts with matter (water) within a certain amount of space. He should also be able to identify various cloud formations and the cause and effects of atmospheric moisture. (Used with permission of Tom Siniard, sixth grade teacher.)

At the end of this unit of instruction, the student should be able to describe the basic structures and functions of each of the plant phyla, to recognize and point out in nature some of the different plants, to point out the different life stages of some plants, and to explain the reproductive processes of some plants. (Used with permission of Jack Bordewick, eighth grade teacher.)

E. IDENTIFY, REVISE, OR DEVELOP STUDENT BEHAVIORAL OBJECTIVES OF THE SCHOOL COURSES

Student behavioral objectives are very specific statements of outcomes of instruction. They state exactly what the learner should be like or should be able to do at the end of instruction. According to Popham and Baker (1967), in order to determine if an objective is stated in behavioral terms, there should be

1. Observable student behavior

   or

2. A product of student behavior.

The term behavioral objective is often used interchangeably with such terms as performance objective, measurable objective, specific objective, and instructional objective. They all seem to be asking the same question, "Can it be determined or specifically measured what the learner has done when the objective is completed?"

Student behavioral objectives are more specific and detailed than terminal objectives. They are more a daily classroom objective, stating many of the minor as well as major things students should be able to do after instruction.

Note: These writers prefer using the word *should* instead of *will* in writing objectives, because in any so-called "average" group of students there will, no doubt, be some who cannot achieve all the objectives. If the objective has been written, "the students will," what about those who do not? Who is to be criticized? The teacher??

Examples:

Student Behavioral Objectives

After the completion of this unit, the student should be able to:

1. List three factors that affect the rate of evaporation of water from an object.
2. Demonstrate the causes and effects of evaporation and condensation.
3. Formulate a hypothesis that explains the increase in air pressure inside a sealed jar in which water vapor has been added to the air. (Used with permission of Tom Siniard, sixth grade teacher.)

Student Behavioral Objectives

After the completion of this unit, the student should be able to:

1. Describe some of the basic structures and functions of algae, fungi, lichens, and mosses.
2. Give reasons why algae, fungi, lichens, and mosses are considered by scientists to be just as important in nature as higher plants.
3. Describe in detail several general characteristics of the vascular plants. (Used with permission of Jack Bordewick, eighth grade teacher.)

To show how the course terminal objectives and student behavioral objectives fit together, the two examples are combined as follows. All of the student behavioral objectives for both units are included. These are objectives developed by teachers and used with their permission.

Science 6 — Unit Two
Course Terminal Objectives

At the end of this unit, the student should be able to state how energy interacts with matter (water) within a certain amount of space. He should also be able to identify various cloud formations and the causes and effects of atmospheric moisture.

Student Behavioral Objectives

After the completion of this unit, the student should be able to:

1. List three factors that affect the rate of evaporation of water from an object.
2. Demonstrate the causes and effects of evaporation and condensation.
3. Formulate a hypothesis that explains the increase in air pressure inside a sealed jar in which water vapor has been added to the air.
4. Infer why air pressure does not increase when water vapor is added to an open container.
5. Identify relative humidity and make readings using a psychrometer.
6. Define dew point as the temperature at which water vapor in the air begins to condense.
7. Explain that frost is water vapor that has condensed to form ice and that frost

forms only on objects that cool below freezing.

8. Distinguish and name several common types of clouds and the kind of weather associated with each type.

9. Make and use simple versions of weather instruments and make changes in barometer readings with changes in the weather. (Used with permission of Tom Siniard, sixth grade teacher.)

Biological Science Plant Life Unit
Eighth Grade
Terminal Objectives

At the end of this unit of instruction, the student should be able to describe the basic structures and functions of each of the plant phyla, to recognize and point out in nature some of the different plants, to point out the different life stages of some plants, and to explain the reproductive processes of some plants.

Student Behavioral Objectives

1. Describe some of the basic structures and functions of algae, fungi, lichen, and mosses.

2. Give reasons why algae, fungi, lichens, and mosses are considered by scientists to be just as important in nature as higher plants.

3. Describe in detail several general characteristics of the vascular plants.

4. Recognize and name some of the types of vascular plants.

5. Name and describe certain structures which are characteristic of ferns and others which are characteristic of gymnosperms.

6. Point out, in illustrations or in the field, examples of the different stages in the life cycles of ferns and of gymnosperms.

7. List the characteristics of flowering plants and explain how flowering plants differ from other groups of plants.

8. Describe the differences between monocotyledons and dicotyledons.

9. List and describe the basic life functions of the flowering plants.

10. State the importance of flowering plants in providing food for man and other animals.

11. Recognize and point out the various parts of a typical flower and explain the functions of each part in the reproductive process. (Used with permission of Jack Bordewick, eighth grade teacher.)

As can be seen from these unit examples, a course terminal objective may consist of a summarized statement of student behavioral objectives. Teachers probably could, and theoretically should, write the terminal objectives first, then, develop student behavioral objectives from them. However, these writers have found it works very well, and is sometimes necessary, to write the behavioral objectives of a unit or chapter first, and then summarize those objectives into terminal objectives. These writers have also found that behavioral objectives of a chapter can be blended into one or two terminal objectives. This means that for a course, there will usually be 8, 10, 12, or possibly 15 course terminal objectives. That is a manageable number of objectives for each course, and the main reason for consolidating objectives into course terminal objectives. With a few terminal objectives, a course can be seen as a whole instead of as bits and pieces, and therefore be better analyzed and evaluated.

Although it is not within the scope of this Handbook, no work with behavioral objectives would be complete without referring to the *Taxonomy of Educational Objectives* (Bloom, 1956, Krathwohl, 1964, Simpson, 1972). The *Taxonomy* is a classification scheme used to identify and define instructional objectives. It includes both specific and general categories of instruction. It helps to determine the level, value and worth of objectives, and therefore, helps to guard against objectives being written to cover only the simple and trivial content, which is sometimes a criticism of behavioral objectives.

The Taxonomy of Educational Objectives is divided into three parts: the cognitive, affective, and psychomotor domains. Each of these is then divided into subparts which include almost all learning outcomes that come from instruction. For further information on the *Taxonomy*, refer to the reference section.

If goals and objectives need to be developed for new programs later in this curriculum planning process, the planner should refer back to this step as a guide.

REFERENCES

Ainsworth, C.S. "Curricular Aims and the Analysis of Needs Statements." *British Journal of Educational Studies*, October, 1976, *24*, 219-232.

Bailey, George D. and Littrell, J. Harvey. "Blueprint for Curriculum Development Establishing a Systematic Design." *NASSP Bulletin*, March, 1981, *65*, 29-32.

Bloom, B. S., (Ed.), and others. *Taxonomy of Educational Objectives: Handbook I, Cognitive Domain*. New York: David McKay, 1956.

Bordewick, Jack. "Course Terminal Objectives and Student Behavioral Objectives." Unpublished course work, Johnson, KS, 1978.

Budnik, Thomas J. "An Estimate of the Reliability of a Technique of Increasing Educational Accountability through Goal Analysis Involving Community, Staff, and Students." *The Journal of Educational Research*, May/June, 1978, *71*, 251-261.

Burns, Richard W. *New Approaches to Behavioral Objectives*. Dubuque, IA: Wm. C. Brown, 1972.

Bushnell, David S. "A Systematic Strategy for School Renewal." *Educational Technology*, February, 1972, 27-33.

Doherty, Victor W. and Peters, Linda B. "Goals and Objectives in Educational Planning and Evaluation." *Educational Leadership*, May, 1981, *38*, 606-611.

Doll, Ronald C. *Curriculum Improvement* (4th ed.). Boston: Allyn and Bacon, 1978.

Educational Innovators Press. *Developing and Writing Performance Objectives*. Tucson, AZ: Educational Innovators Press, 1971.

Fairbanks, Dwight W. "Copy This Sensible Approach to Setting Goals for Your Schools." *The American School Board Journal*, August, 1976, *163*, 34.

Feldhusen, John F.; Ames, Russell E., Jr.; and Linden, Kathryn W. "Designing Instruction to Achieve Higher Level Goals and Objectives." *Educational Technology*, October, 1974, *14*, 21-23.

Gray, Frank and Burns, Margaret L. "Does 'Management by Objectives' Work in Education?" *Educational Leadership*, March, 1979, *36*, 414-417.

Gronlund, Norman E. *Stating Behavioral Objectives for Classroom Instruction*. New York: Macmillan, 1978.

Hartman, Arlene. "Reaching Consensus Using the Delphi Technique." *Educational Leadership*, March, 1981, 495-497.

Hostrop, Richard W. *Managing Education for Results*. Homewood, IL: ETC Publications, 1973.

House, Ernest R. (Ed.). *School Evaluation*. Berkeley, CA: McCutchan, 1973.

Knief, Lotus M. "Objectives Are Not the Place to Begin." *Educational Technology*, February, 1974, *14*, 37-39.

Krathwohl, D. R., (Ed.), and others. *Taxonomy of Educational Objectives: Handbook II, Affective Domain*. New York: David McKay, 1964.

Mager, Robert F. *Preparing Instructional Objectives*. Palo Alto, CA: Fearon Publishers, 1962.

McGreal, Thomas L. "Helping Teachers Set Goals." *Educational Leadership*, February, 1980, *37*, 414-419.

Nault, William H. *Typical Course of Study*. Chicago: Field Enterprises Educational Corp., 1978.

Neagley, Ross L. and Evans, N. Dean. *Handbook for Effective Curriculum Development*. Englewood Cliffs, NJ: Prentice-Hall, 1967.

Newfield, John W., and Duet, Claude P. "Implications of Quality of Life for Goal Setting Tasks of Curriculum Workers." *Education*, Winter, 1976, *97*, 126-135.

Oliver, Albert I. *Curriculum Improvement: A Guide to Problems, Principles, and Process* (2nd ed.). New York: Harper and Row, 1977.

Phi Delta Kappa. *Educational Goals and Objectives*. Bloomington, IN: Phi Delta Kappa, 1978.

Popham, W. James and Baker, Eva L. *Educational Objectives*. Los Angeles: Vimcet Associates, 1967.

Pratt, David. *Curriculum Design and Development*. New York: Harcourt Brace Jovanovich, 1980.

Reed, James and Bakken, John. "The Classroom Teacher and Curriculum Development—A New Approach Suggested." *Man/Society/Technology*, December, 1972, *32*, 147-150.

Saylor, Galen J.; Alexander, William M.; and Lewis, Arthur J. *Curriculum Planning for Better Teaching and Learning* (4th ed.). Chicago: Holt, Rinehart and Winston, 1981.

Simpson, E. J. "The Classification of Educational Objectives in the Psychomotor Domain." *The Psychomotor Domain*. Vol. 3. Washington: Gryphon House, 1972.

Siniard, Tom. "Course Terminal Objectives and Student Behavioral Objectives." Unpublished course work, Johnson, KS, 1978.

Tankard, George C., Jr. *Curriculum Improvement: An Administrator's Guide*. West Nyack, NY: Parker, 1974.

Thompson, Donald L. and Borsari, Leonard R. "An Overview of Management by Objectives for Guidance and Counseling Services." *The School Counselor*, June, 1978, *25*, 172-177.

Tyler, Ralph W. "Specific Approaches to Curriculum Development." In James R. Gress and David E. Purpel (Eds.), *Curriculum, An Introduction to the Field*. Berkeley: McCutchan, 1978.

VanEvery, Donald F. "Developing Curriculum Through Goals and Objectives." *Croft Curriculum Trends*, May, 1976.

Wiles, Jon and Bondi, Joseph, Jr. *Curriculum Development*. Columbus: Charles E. Merrill, 1979.

Williams, C. Ray. "In the Beginning. . .Goals." *Theory Into Practice*, August, 1976, *15*, 86-89.

Williams, William H. "Major Steps in Developing Curriculum." *Industrial Education*, September, 1971, *60*, 79-81.

Zahorik, John A. "Learning Activities: The Objectives—Seeking Function." *The Elementary School Journal*, September, 1976, *77*, 50-56.

Zahorik, John A. "The Virtue of Vagueness in Instructional Objectives." *The Elementary School Journal*, April, 1976, *76*, 411-419.

STEP III

PLAN AND ORGANIZE THE RESOURCES AND CONSTRAINTS

OF CURRICULUM DEVELOPMENT

ONCE THE CURRICULUM NEED HAS BEEN DETERMINED AND STATED, AND GOALS AND OBJECTIVES IDENTIFIED OR DEVELOPED, THE NEXT STEP IS TO DO SOMETHING TO MEET THAT NEED. THIS WILL, IN MOST CASES, INVOLVE A CURRICULUM STUDY OF SOME TYPE AND THAT IN TURN NECESSITATES PLANNING AND ORGANIZING POSSIBLE RE-SOURCES AND CONSTRAINTS FOR THE STUDY. STEPS III, IV, AND V ARE DESIGNED TO GUIDE THE PRELIMINARY PREPARATION FOR SUCH CURRICULUM STUDIES.

III. PLAN AND ORGANIZE THE RESOURCES AND CONSTRAINTS OF CURRICULUM DEVELOPMENT

	CONSIDERING IT	PLANNING IT	DOING IT	COMPLETED	NOT NEEDED
A. OBTAIN COMMITMENT OF BOARD OF EDUCATION FOR CURRICULUM DEVELOPMENT					
B. DETERMINE AND SECURE NECESSARY FINANCES FOR THE CURRICULUM STUDY					
C. DETERMINE AVAILABILITY OF QUALIFIED PERSONNEL WITHIN THE SCHOOL SYSTEM FOR THE CURRICULUM STUDY					
D. ALLOT SUFFICIENT TIME FOR THE CURRICULUM STUDY					
E. DETERMINE AVAILABILITY OF FACILITIES, EQUIPMENT AND MATERIALS FOR THE CURRICULUM STUDY					
F. IDENTIFY POSSIBLE CONSTRAINTS OR BARRIERS TO THE CURRICULUM STUDY AND PLAN HOW TO OVERCOME THEM					

III. PLAN AND ORGANIZE THE RESOURCES AND CONSTRAINTS OF CURRICULUM DEVELOPMENT

Once the problem or need has been established and the goals identified or developed, the next step is to determine if the board of education will support a study to solve the problem. Some of the elements which need to be considered as to availability are facilities, equipment, and materials. At this stage a tentative budget is planned, and personnel to be involved are identified. Possible constraints or barriers to the study are also recognized and plans made to overcome them.

These are preliminary plans and have to be somewhat tentative because once the study begins, circumstances tend to change which many times require a revision of plans. These preliminary plans should provide for implementation and evaluation of any new program on a pilot basis. If a new program is adopted and placed in the curriculum on a permanent basis, this step should be used again as a guide to plan and organize resources for the implementation and evaluation of that program.

A. OBTAIN COMMITMENT OF BOARD OF EDUCATION FOR CURRICULUM DEVELOPMENT

First of all, the board of education must be committed to curriculum planning and development and also must be committed to the point of furnishing resources for doing it. Once this occurs, a policy needs to be designed by the administrative staff with input from the total staff. A faculty hearing should be held before the final draft of the policy is submitted to the board for its approval.

The board policy on curriculum planning and development should include a description of how the school system will be organized for development of the curriculum. That is, it should include who has primary responsibility for planning the curriculum, which standing committees will be used and what their functions will be, and when the curricula will be reviewed throughout the system. By approving such a policy, the board of education is committing itself to curriculum development. These writers recommend studying the policy of two or three school systems of similar size for ideas.

B. DETERMINE AND SECURE NECESSARY FINANCES FOR THE CURRICULUM STUDY

In the beginning, the amount of money needed for a curriculum study is difficult to project. Therefore, instead of attempting to establish a detailed budget at first, it may be necessary to set a certain amount of money aside for the curriculum study and use whatever is needed. As the study progresses, the cost estimates can become more specific. These first costs, as well as the estimates for future costs of the study, may well determine if the curriculum planning and development continues. This is one reason a commitment by the board of education regarding curriculum development is so important.

Once the study gets underway, provisions should be made as needed for the following:

• Administrative and supervisory staff.

- Time for staff meetings.
- Released time for teachers—substitute teachers.
- Travel and visitation expenses.
- Summer salaries and work done outside school hours.
- Curriculum materials.
- Consultants.
- Inservice training.
- Clerical work.
- Paper and printing costs.
- Whatever is reasonably necessary to complete the study.

C. DETERMINE AVAILABILITY OF QUALIFIED PERSONNEL WITHIN THE SCHOOL SYSTEM FOR THE CURRICULUM STUDY

Next to having the finances for curriculum planning, the most important need is personnel who are willing to give the time and effort to carry out the task. Curriculum planning and development is slow, hard, tedious, and often thankless work. However, it does not have to be if the curriculum leaders know their jobs. The leaders are responsible for setting the mood and atmosphere of curriculum development. Their specific roles will be defined in Steps IV and V of this Handbook. For this stage of the planning, it is sufficient to determine if individuals are available who are willing to look at what is presently being done and what might be possible.

The first individual needed for even the preliminary planning is someone to be in charge. If the system has a curriculum coordinator or someone responsible for curriculum development, that is the person who should be selected. If there is no such individual in the system, a responsible and respected person (often a principal in small systems) should be made the leader with the *authority* as well as *responsibility* for doing whatever is necessary to determine the curriculum planning that should and can be done. The same types of individuals as those chosen for leaders, if possible, should be selected to help with curriculum planning and development. The number needed will vary with the type of planning being considered. Planning and curriculum committees should be large enough for ample representation of those affected, and yet not so large that the work is hindered. The specifics of curriculum committees will be dealt with in Step IV of this Handbook.

The main thing to consider at this point is that adequate personnel be available for curriculum planning and that provisions be made for their release from regular responsibilities.

D. ALLOT SUFFICIENT TIME FOR THE CURRICULUM STUDY

Finding time for curriculum planning is very difficult but very important. The amount of time needed has to be estimated and, at best, is only a guess. It is even more difficult to estimate the amount of time necessary for this preliminary stage of planning; therefore, the commitment from the school administration should be for whatever time is reasonably needed. In addition to the board's commitment, the staff must also be committed. This means that the board of education will provide some school time, and the participating staff members must be willing to give some of their time. Providing time for curriculum planning includes:

1. Released time for curriculum planning to:
   a. Attend planned meetings, review the literature, research, and write.
   b. Visit other school systems, attend conferences, meetings and workshops.
2. Reasonable teaching loads for teachers involved in curriculum studies.
3. Inservice days when needed.
4. Summer work when needed; teachers may be willing to work for substitute pay since students are not present.

E. DETERMINE AVAILABILITY OF FACILITIES, EQUIPMENT, AND MATERIALS FOR THE CURRICULUM STUDY

Most of the facilities, equipment, and materials needed to organize for curriculum planning are already in the school system and available for use. Such things as meeting rooms, school records, professional materials, software, and hardware are usually accessible and can be used without much difficulty, especially if the administrative staff is totally committed to the curriculum planning. It is a good idea at this point, however, to make a quick check of these and note if there are any that are not available. If not, the planner should determine if they can be made available. Facilities, equipment, and materials become much more crucial during the design and implementation stages of curriculum planning and will be defined in those steps of this Handbook.

One facility which helps to provide materials and equipment, and usually needs some attention at this stage of the planning, is the curriculum library, resource center, media center, or professional library. This is a time when someone, usually librarian, should be assigned as the one in charge of ordering needed information, materials, and equipment. That individual should attend curriculum committee meetings when necessary materials and equipment are determined. This is also a time when funds from the curriculum planning project can be used in the curriculum library.

Some of the services provided by the curriculum library and the individual in charge are to:

- Develop a list of materials and information in the library which are required for the study.
- Order those materials and information not in the library and needed for the curriculum study.
- Help coordinate all materials and information for the curriculum study.

F. IDENTIFY POSSIBLE CONSTRAINTS OR BARRIERS TO THE CURRICULUM STUDY AND PLAN HOW TO OVERCOME THEM

A review of past curriculum development within the school district will be helpful in identifying possible constraints or barriers to the curriculum study. These barriers to curriculum planning may take the form of tradition, attitudes, laws, policies, lack of needed resources (including finances), staff, time, physical environment or anything which helps to maintain the status quo. These do not have to be constraints; however, they can be resources just as well. The more tenured teachers and administrators are likely to be the best sources for identifying possible constraints to curriculum planning and development; however, the thoughts of the less tenured teachers should not be overlooked. Retrieval of information and material is a very important resource as well as a barrier to curriculum planning at times. This does not have to be; however, because with the help of library personnel, systematic acquisition procedures can be used to acquire almost all that is needed.

These possible constraints should be defined, as well as possible ways to keep them from becoming barriers to curriculum development. However, caution should be taken not to over-emphasize possible constraints; or curriculum development may never begin.

SOME CAUTIONS FOR CURRICULUM DEVELOPMENT

- First, curriculum development must have the support and backing of school administrators, their total commitment.
- A proposed curriculum innovation or change should be systematically studied, planned, and in most cases, piloted on a small scale before implementing it into the entire curriculum.
- A proposed curriculum study or change may take more time and money than first planned.
- A change in the curriculum can set off a chain reaction causing problems in other areas of the curriculum. When something is added, something probably has to be taken out and vice versa.
- An innovation should not be started the minute it is encountered, nor should it be eliminated the minute it is suggested. The first reaction usually is that it is not possible to do that in this school system. "It has never been done that way here." The planners need to study all possible implications and problems before attempting to implement something new into the curriculum.
- No more than one or two areas of the curriculum should be studied or changed at one time. These areas need to be well identified, systematically studied, and the study completed, including an evaluation of what was done. Everyone involved and/or with a vested interest should be kept informed about the progress of the study. Once the study is completed, individuals involved should be recognized and praised before starting another study.
- Once a new program or change of any kind is set in motion, it has to be maintained. For example, adequate time for staff planning and inservice training of staff must be moni-

tored and provided as needed. Any problems that arise with the new program should be resolved as quickly as possible.

REFERENCES

Buell, Clayton E. "Guidelines for Curriculum Development." *Educational Leadership*, December, 1968, *26*, 293-297.

Bushnell, David S. "A Systematic Strategy for School Renewal." *Educational Technology*, February, 1972, 27-33.

Doll, Ronald C. *Curriculum Improvement* (4th ed.). Boston: Allyn and Bacon, 1978.

English, Fenwick W. "Management Practice as a Key to Curriculum Leadership." *Educational Leadership*, March, 1979, 408-413.

Kratz, Robert N. "Educational Planning: If You're Not Ahead, You're Behind." *NASSP Bulletin*, November, 1972, *56*, 26-31.

Neagley, Ross L. and Evans, N. Dean. *Handbook for Effective Curriculum Development*. Englewood Cliffs, NJ: Prentice-Hall, 1967.

Pratt, David. *Curriculum, Design and Development*. New York: Harcourt Brace Jovanovich, 1980.

Saylor, Galen J.; Alexander, William M.; and Lewis, Arthur J. *Curriculum Planning for Better Technique and Learning* (4th ed.). Chicago: Holt, Rinehart and Winston, 1981.

Tankard, George C., Jr. *Curriculum Improvement: An Administrator's Guide*. West Nyack, NY: Parker, 1974.

Tyler, Ralph W. "Specific Approaches to Curriculum Development." In James R. Gress and David E. Purpel (Eds.), *Curriculum, An Introduction to the Field*. Berkeley: McCutchan, 1978.

Wickert, Jack J. "Criteria for Curriculum Development." *Educational Leadership*, January, 1973, *30*, 339-342.

Wiles, Jon and Bondi, Joseph, Jr. *Curriculum Development*. Columbus: Charles E. Merrill, 1979.

STEP IV

STATE THE FUNCTIONS OF AND SELECT CURRICULUM COMMITTEES USED

FOR CURRICULUM PLANNING AND DEVELOPMENT

Curriculum committees have long been advocated and used in curriculum planning and development. Today there is a strong emphasis on using committees to make curriculum planning a cooperative effort including teachers, administrators, parents, citizens, and to some extent, students.

The four most used curriculum committees are identified and described in this section of the Handbook. These committees are known by different names; but whatever title is given them, they seem to be the four basic committees used to plan and develop school curricula. An attempt has been made to describe the organization and function of these committees. However, all of these committees, and functions of each, would *not* necessarily be used by a school system involved in a curriculum study. In fact, it would be unusual if a system, especially a small system, did use all of them for a single study. Large school systems tend to have standing committees, and therefore, use all of them more than the small schools. *For a small system, one curriculum committee may serve as two or even three of the committees described here.* This explanation of the curriculum committees is to serve as a guide, a point of departure, not as the exact and only way to organize and use them.

IV. **STATE THE FUNCTIONS OF AND SELECT CURRICULUM COMMITTEES USED FOR CURRICULUM PLANNING AND DEVELOPMENT**

	CONSIDERING IT	PLANNING IT	DOING IT	COMPLETED	NOT NEEDED
A. CITIZENS' ADVISORY COMMITTEE 1. STATE THE MAIN FUNCTIONS AND DUTIES OF THE CITIZENS' ADVISORY COMMITTEE FOR CURRICULUM STUDY					
2. SELECT COMMITTEE MEMBERS					
B. CURRICULUM COUNCIL 1. STATE THE MAIN FUNCTIONS AND DUTIES OF THE CURRICULUM COUNCIL FOR CURRICULUM STUDY					
2. SELECT COMMITTEE MEMBERS					
C. SUBJECT AREA CURRICULUM COMMITTEE(S) 1. STATE THE MAIN FUNCTIONS AND DUTIES OF THE COMMITTEE(S) FOR CURRICULUM STUDY					
2. SELECT COMMITTEE MEMBERS					
D. STUDY COMMITTEE(S) (AD HOC) 1. STATE THE MAIN FUNCTIONS AND DUTIES OF THE COMMITTEE(S) FOR CURRICULUM STUDY					
2. SELECT COMMITTEE MEMBERS					

IV. **STATE THE MAIN FUNCTIONS OF AND SELECT CURRICULUM COMMITTEES USED FOR CURRICULUM PLANNING DEVELOPMENT**

Note: It may not be necessary or advisable to use all of these committees every time curriculum development is done. For those that are not necessary, check the "Not Needed" space and go on to the next committee. Checking "Not Needed" means that the committee has been considered but is not necessary for this particular study.

A. **CITIZENS' ADVISORY COMMITTEE**

1. **STATE THE MAIN FUNCTIONS AND DUTIES OF THE CITIZENS' ADVISORY COMMITTEE FOR CURRICULUM STUDY**

   A great deal of caution should be exercised in organizing and using the citizens' advisory committee. Its functions should be very well established and clearly stated. The functions should be *advisory only* and should be clearly stated by written policy. This guards against groups attempting to make policy, since the board of education determines policy. It is advisable to have an agenda of specific topics for each meeting; this helps prevent it from turning into a gripe session. If it is a district-wide committee, the superintendent may want to have well informed educators from the district present when the committee meets to help answer questions about what is presently happening and why.

   Main Functions:
   - Serves as a sounding board for the aspirations and expectations of the community.
   - Identifies specific educational needs.
   - Identifies specific strengths and weaknesses of the present curriculum.
   - Assists in the evaluation of curriculum studies.
   - Suggests solutions to educational problems.
   - All of these assist in determining goals and objectives of the school system.

   Advisory Committees can also be used to:
   - Influence public attitudes in support of a curriculum change.
   - Interpret educational conditions to the community, seeking their support for improvement.
   - Harmonize differences between school officials and the community.

2. **SELECT COMMITTEE MEMBERS**
   These committee members may be selected in the following manner:
   - Appointment by the superintendent and/or other administrators, possibly by the board of education.
   - Invitation from the board of education to community interest groups, possibly by asking them to name a representative from a civic, religious, labor, business, industrial, or parents' group. Caution: The committee can get too large.
   - Request names from pupils, teachers, parents, citizens, and organized groups; then

a special committee of citizens can develop a preferential list from these names, and the final choice is made from the preferential list by the administration and/or board of education.

If system-wide, the committee should be chaired by the superintendent or possibly by one of his/her assistants and should be as broadly representative of the community as possible with an optimum size of 15-25 members. Qualifications for memberships are as follows:

(1) Willing and able to attend meetings.

(2) Respected by those whom they represent.

(3) Capable of communicating the ideas of those whom they represent.

B. CURRICULUM COUNCIL

1. STATE THE MAIN FUNCTIONS AND DUTIES OF THE CURRICULUM COUNCIL FOR CURRICULUM STUDY

Since the curriculum council usually involves personnel from the entire school district, and also since it initiates and is a clearing house for studies, experiments, and innovations, more information is included concerning it than for the other committees. *Main Functions:*

- Formulate and recommend general policy for system-wide curriculum development (including how the council itself will function). Duties and functions need to be contained within the policy of the board of education.

- Coordinate system-wide curriculum planning and study. This includes establishing curriculum committees and the *major areas of curriculum to be studied each year*. It serves as a clearing house for curriculum problems and ideas. The full council should not spend a great amount of time trying to decide if a problem should or should not be accepted for study or be assigned immediately to a committee for solution. Instead, the council should organize a study group to study the merits of the problem; then with detailed information and a recommendation from that study group, the council should make a decision as to whether or not it should become involved in the problem. Unless precautions are taken, councils can become involved in and burdened with problems that are not their concern.

- Facilitate communications. The council serves as a communications link between various components of the school system by keeping itself informed of curriculum development activities and disseminating the results of these activities to all concerned. Newsletters, bulletins, minutes of the council meetings, and council members reporting to the various faculties are the usual ways of disseminating information. Provisions also must be made for the staff to present their ideas and concerns directly to the council or to the representatives who serve on the council.

- Serve as a guide for curriculum development activities. When individuals, as well as planning and study committees, present progress reports at council meetings, assistance and guidance is provided to them by the curriculum council. The exchange of ideas and information also assists in the communications process.

- Advise the administration. All curriculum revisions and recommendations are approved by the council before being submitted to the superintendent. These recommendations also inform administrators of views of the staff, curriculum needs of the system, and possible methods for improving the curriculum.
- Recommend and assist in organizing permanent curriculum committees, K-12 subject area committees, or any others needed.
- Develop school district system-wide philosophy and goals.
- Assess and evaluate school district system-wide curriculum development from year to year.
    (These functions by a curriculum council will usually prevent mandates from the administration and also help to assure a systematic plan for curriculum planning, study, and change.)

SOME MAJOR TASKS OF THE CURRICULUM COUNCIL IN CARRYING OUT THE MAIN FUNCTIONS

- Surveying curriculum needs, doing a needs assessment when necessary.
- Screening curriculum problems.
- Initiating and sponsoring curriculum studies (getting action started).
- Assigning problems to planning, subject area, or study committees.
- Coordinating curriculum studies.
- Considering committee reports and making recommendations.
- Locating materials and resources for curricular activities and studies.
- Assessing and evaluating curricular activities and studies.
- Coordinating and sponsoring in-service education programs.
- Promoting good public relations.

POSSIBLE ISSUES TO BE CONSIDERED BY THE COUNCIL

- Policy statements which guide the staff.
- Teaching of controversial issues.
- Use of instructional media.
- Most efficient use of existing resources.
- Identification of needed resources and facilities, only as they directly relate to curriculum.
- In-service programs.
- Additions, revisions, and deletions from the existing curriculum.
- Testing policies and procedures.
- Absences and dropouts.

SOME GUIDELINES FOR CURRICULUM COUNCILS

- Plan curriculum council meetings well in advance, checking for conflicts.

- Be sure to begin and close meetings on time.
- Should not meet longer than one and one-half hours, or two hours at the most.
- Prepare an agenda and stick to it; send it out *at least two or three days* before the meeting.
- Reserve a place on the agenda for input from representatives.

Curriculum Council should:

- Meet once a month, more or less as necessary.
- Meet in the same place (central location) and make it as routine as possible.
- Have something serious to consider (usually instructional problems) so members can see progress.
- Be chaired by the curriculum coordinator or some other administrator. Administrative and supervisory council members must, however, avoid using their status in pressing their point of view too much.
- Consider proposals in light of the district's philosophy, goals, staff, budget, students, and various alternatives.
- Appoint a small group within the council (planning group, study group) to study the problem and suggest a way to approach it, when problems are identified and it is not immediately clear what to do first.
- Must not be confused with the professional negotiations committee. The curriculum should never be negotiated. Only the method by which the curriculum is to be developed can be negotiated.
- The top administrators must be committed (with board support) to and supportive of the council or it is not going to be very effective. They must create a climate and environment in which the council can work. According to Feyereisen *et al* (1970), they can accomplish this by:
  - (1) Respecting the ability of the council to produce satisfactory solutions to problems.
  - (2) Fostering a sense of group purpose among the staff members of the system.
  - (3) Providing the resources needed for effective operation of the curriculum council.
  - (4) Accepting and seriously considering all recommendations submitted by the curriculum council.
- Curriculum council guidelines must have for their central theme, "The welfare of students."
- Provisions should be made to permit and enable teachers, administrators, students, and community members to present proposals to the council.
- All major proposals to the council should be in writing and should include a rationale. A proponent of the proposal should be present to further explain it if necessary.
- Council members have to be willing to work, much of the time without pay, to consider proposals, to draw up guidelines for the proposals, and to make proposals

of their own.

2. SELECT COMMITTEE MEMBERS

Principals should nominate individuals, and the superintendent or his designee should make the final selection. The members may also be appointed or elected by their schools or representative groups.

The curriculum council should be chaired by the curriculum coordinator. In case there is no curriculum coordinator, the chairperson should be selected by the superintendent and should be an administrator or supervisor. The curriculum council needs an authority figure as chairperson. The council should be representative of all levels of the total school system and not more than 25 in number. Qualifications for membership include:

(1) Interest.
(2) Willingness to work.
(3) Respect from colleagues.
(4) Knowledge in the area of curriculum.
(5) At least one year's experience in the school.
(6) Schedule that allows him/her to be present at the meetings.

C. SUBJECT AREA CURRICULUM COMMITTEE(S) — K-12

Subject areas include the major disciplines of the curriculum such as mathematics, language arts, science, and social sciences. These committees may be K-12 committees in the smaller systems, K-6, and 7-12, or even broken down into more committees in the larger school systems.

1. STATE THE MAIN FUNCTIONS AND DUTIES OF THESE COMMITTEES FOR CURRICULUM STUDY

Main Functions:

- Coordinate curriculum development within the subject area. This function could include the development and coordination of general objectives of the subject area.
- Coordinate the selection of textbooks and instructional materials.
- Organize, guide and evaluate experimental programs within the subject area.
- Organize subject study committees as needed.
- Hold periodic all-staff meetings of the subject or subject area being studied:
    (1) For continuous progress reports.
    (2) To bring in consultants.
- Make recommendations to the curriculum council.
- Coordinate the writing of curriculum guides.
- Study specific problems related to their subjects and subject areas.

2. SELECT COMMITTEE MEMBERS

Curriculum coordinators and principals may identify, recommend, and/or appoint competent teachers, especially if there is no council. Teachers could be elected or appointed by their representative groups, or just volunteer; however, they should have some teaching experience and be willing to serve (work).

If the system is large enough to have subject area curriculum coordinators, that individual should be the chairperson. If not, some other administrator or supervisor should chair the committee. These writers are finding more and more of these committees being chaired by administrators. The chairperson could be elected from within the committee keeping in mind that there should be equal representation of elementary secondary people chairing the committee. This individual should also be a member of the curriculum council. Members may include:

(1) Teachers from all levels in that subject area.

(2) Students could be on this committee, but probably better for them not to be. Provisions should be made for their input through student groups.

(3) Lay people could be members, but probably better for them not to be. There should be provisions for their input as needed.

D. STUDY COMMITTEE(S) (AD HOC)

1. STATE THE MAIN FUNCTIONS AND DUTIES OF THE COMMITTEE(S) FOR CURRICULUM STUDY

The main function of this committee is to study whatever they are appointed or assigned to do. These are Ad Hoc committees which means they are organized to study a certain problem and then are dissolved. Therefore, it is difficult to state what the main function of this committee will be; however, the main functions may include some of the following:

- Determine what is now being done:
    (1) Note objectives, content and available instructional material.
    (2) Coordinate objectives of grade levels and courses.
    (3) Consider students needs, interests, and abilities.
- Determine what could be, what is possible, and what is new in the field.
    (1) Review the literature, especially the research on the subject and examine national curriculum projects or any innovative programs. Review latest theories of scholars in the field. Visit other schools and converse with other educators; call in consultants as needed.
- What should be, or what they recommend for their situation, *probably on a pilot basis*.
    (1) After studying what is presently being done in the curriculum of this subject area and new ideas in the field, recommend what should be tried, if anything, to improve the curriculum. New curricula should almost

always be tried on a pilot basis first.

- Develop a curriculum guide if something different is to be tried. This guide should be constructed so materials can be added and deleted. Any significant changes to the guide should be approved by the appropriate curriculum committee. (See Appendix A for instructions on writing a curriculum guide.)

2. SELECT COMMITTEE MEMBERS

The committee members may be selected by the subject area curriculum committee. Curriculum coordinators and principals may identify, recommend, and/or appoint competent teachers. Teachers could be elected or appointed by their representative groups, or they could volunteer. They should have some teaching experience and be willing to serve (work). Members may include:

(1) As many teachers as possible from each grade or teaching level (primary, intermediate, junior high, senior high) in the given subject or topic being considered.

(2) Administrators, although probably not, unless as chairpersons of the committees.

(3) Lay people or students who could be called in as needed, however, probably not as members of the committee.

REFERENCES

Alexander, William M. "Citizen Advisory Committees on Curriculum." *Curriculum Trends*, April, 1975.

Bulach, Cletus R. "An Organizational Plan for Curriculum Development." *Educational Leadership*, January, 1978, *35*, 308-312.

Doll, Ronald C. *Curriculum Improvement* (4th ed.). Boston: Allyn and Bacon, 1978.

Feyereisen, Kathryn V.; Fiorino, A. John; and Nowak, Arlene T. *Supervision and Curriculum Renewal: A Systems Approach*. New York: Appleton-Century-Crofts, 1970.

Fisher, Allen. "Advisory Committees—Does Anybody Want Their Advice?" *Educational Leadership*, December 1979, *37*, 254-255.

Frymier, Jack R. and Hawn, Horace C. *Curriculum Improvement for Better Schools*. Worthington, OH: Charles A. Jones, 1970.

Jackson, Shirley A. "The Curriculum Council: New Hope, New Promise." *Educational Leadership*, May, 1972, *29*, 690-694.

Neagley, Ross L. and Evans, N. Dean. *Handbook for Effective Curriculum Development*. Englewood Cliffs, NJ: Prentice-Hall, 1967.

O'Hanlon, James and Wood, Fred H. "Regenerating the Curriculum Committee." *Educational Leadership*, November, 1972, *30*, 157-159.

Pratt, David. *Curriculum, Design and Development*. New York: Harcourt Brace Jovanovich, 1980.

Saylor, Galen J.; Alexander, William M.; and Lewis, Arthur J. *Curriculum Planning for Better Teaching and Learning* (4th ed.). Chicago: Holt, Rinehart and Winston, 1981.

Tankard, George C., Jr. *Curriculum Improvement: An Administrator's Guide*. West Nyack, NY: Parker, 1974.

Wiles, Jon and Bondi, Joseph, Jr. *Curriculum Development*. Columbus: Charles E. Merrill, 1979.

STEP V

PLAN AND STATE THE ROLES AND RESPONSIBILITIES OF PERSONNEL INVOLVED

INDIVIDUALS AT ALL LEVELS, AS WELL AS COMMITTEES, NEED TO BE INVOLVED IN CURRICULUM PLANNING AND DEVELOPMENT. THIS STEP INCLUDES MANY OF THE ACTIVITIES FOR WHICH INDIVIDUALS SHOULD AND CAN BE RESPONSIBLE. HOWEVER, THESE ROLES AND ACTIVITIES ARE NOT ALL INCLUSIVE NOR SHOULD THEY ALL NECESSARILY BE USED IN ANY GIVEN CURRICULUM STUDY. ROLES AND RESPONSIBILITIES THAT ARE APPROPRIATE AND APPLICABLE FOR INDIVIDUALS INVOLVED SHOULD BE USED AS NEEDED FOR A PARTICULAR STUDY.

STEP V

V. **PLAN AND STATE THE ROLES AND RESPONSIBILITIES OF PERSONNEL INVOLVED**

IDENTIFY AND STATE THE ROLE AND RESPONSIBILITY OF THE FOLLOWING INDIVIDUALS FOR THIS CURRICULUM STUDY:

	CONSIDERING IT	PLANNING IT	DOING IT	COMPLETED	NOT NEEDED
A. SUPERINTENDENT					
B. INTERMEDIATE ADMINISTRATOR, IF THERE IS ONE—ASSISTANT SUPERINTENDENT, CURRICULUM COORDINATOR, ELEMENTARY OR SECONDARY DIRECTOR					
C. BUILDING PRINCIPAL					
D. SUBJECT AREA (DISCIPLINE) CURRICULUM COMMITTEE CHAIRPERSON					
E. STUDY COMMITTEE (AD HOC) CHAIRPERSON					
F. TEACHER WHO IS A CURRICULUM COMMITTEE MEMBER					
G. TEACHER WHO IS NOT A CURRICULUM COMMITTEE MEMBER					
H. CONSULTANT—IF ONE IS USED					

47

V. PLAN AND STATE THE ROLES AND RESPONSIBILITIES OF PERSONNEL INVOLVED

A. SUPERINTENDENT

- Makes the decision to do something about, as well as sets the mood for, curriculum development. He/she must give it personal attention if curriculum development is to succeed, especially in smaller districts.
- Delegates the responsibility to some person, usually an intermediate administrator. Small systems may choose a principal or curriculum committee chairperson to be in charge.
- Lets the individual in charge of the curriculum study know what is expected of him/her and the range and limit of his/her authority. This individual should have both *responsibility* and *authority* for the study and know what they are.
- He/she meets periodically with the curriculum committees (except perhaps in large school systems):
    1. First, to explain why the curriculum should be studied and possibly improved.
    2. Then, to follow through, keep informed, lend support, show enthusiasm, and commend good work.
- Must be satisfied with realistic (sometimes little) progress each year. He/she is working with human and institutional behavior.
- Provides for adequate public relations and publicity.
- Interprets curriculum developments to the board of education.

B. INTERMEDIATE ADMINISTRATOR, IF THERE IS ONE—ASSISTANT SUPERINTENDENT, CURRICULUM COORDINATOR, ELEMENTARY OR SECONDARY DIRECTOR

- Intermediate Administrator: This position is between the top administrator and the individual school administrators. This is usually an assistant superintendent, curriculum director or coordinator, or elementary or secondary director position of some type. Small school systems may not have this position; in that case, the principal, or whoever is in charge, assumes these duties.
- Makes sure that his/her *responsibilities* and *authority* are clear. There can be conflict between this individual and the principal.
- Is chairperson of the curriculum council.
- Is a liaison person, attempts to keep everyone who is involved informed, happy and working.
- Commends good work: a personal note, phone call, or a pat on the back will do a lot for attitudes and morale. This is true when the pat comes from anyone in a high authoritative position.
- He/she is a compromiser, chief public relations person, and trouble shooter, who works closely with other curriculum coordinators, principals, and curriculum committees.
- Keeps the superintendent informed so he/she can defend the study. Assumes duties

delegated from the superintendent.
- Accepts responsibility for keeping curriculum development going:
    1. Keeps abreast of the latest general developments affecting curricula in all subject areas.
    2. Maintains contact with resource personnel and materials.
    3. Establishes the budget for curriculum planning and development.
    4. Provides for a professional curriculum library(ies).
    5. Provides for evaluation and feedback of curriculum studies.
- *Note:* These individuals have to be very diplomatic in guiding and directing curriculum development because teachers often do not accept them or understand their roles. Some teachers may not be in accord with their appointment to this position. Others resent them because they represent authority or change which is threatening. Curriculum coordinators do not always know what their roles are; therefore, they should have their roles defined by a job description, if at all possible.

C. BUILDING PRINCIPAL
- Is one of the key individuals (if not the key individual) in any curriculum study. If there are no curriculum committees or coordinators, then the building principal is not only the key person, but probably the only one to lead the study.
- May serve as a member of the curriculum council.
- Works directly with the curriculum coordinator(s), elementary and secondary coordinator(s), subject area coordinator(s), and fellow principals. These are very sensitive relationships and it should be clear who is in charge of the study. Line and staff relationships should be clarified and defined.
- Attempts to keep up-to-date on general curriculum movements for his/her level by: reviewing current literature, attending professional meetings, visiting other schools, and seeking advice of authorities in the field.
- Helps the staff see the need for and accept curriculum studies and possible change. If he/she is behind the study, it will probably succeed; if not, it probably will not be successful. He/she is a key person in keeping the study going, a key person in any curriculum work.
- Helps in attempting to provide reasonable teacher loads, materials, secretarial help, and release time for curriculum study. He/she attempts to employ teachers interested in curriculum development and schedules times so involved teachers can plan together.
- Helps interpret curriculum studies to the faculty in his/her building.
- Follows through and commends good work whenever possible.
- Interprets the curriculum study to visitors, parents, patrons, students, especially those who visit his/her building.
- Evaluates the study in his/her building; this may include some student evaluation of the study.

D. SUBJECT AREA (DISCIPLINE) CURRICULUM COMMITTEE CHAIRPERSON

- These may be K-12 committees in the smaller systems, K-6 and 7-12 or broken down into even more committees in the larger systems. The chairperson should be an administrator, if possible. Administrators usually have more clout to move a committee into action. Subject area curriculum coordinators, in schools that have them, make good chairpersons for this committee. Whoever the chairperson is, the first thing he/she should do is determine what his/her role is and get a job description, if possible. This includes what he/she is to do as well as the authority and limitations.
- Should be a member of the curriculum council, unless it is a large system where there are too many chairpersons for all to be on the council.
- Visits and works with classroom teachers in this subject area. Since this is often a sensitive relationship, he/she visits the teacher's classroom only with permission.
- Plans and works with principals and curriculum coordinators from both elementary and secondary levels. This is also a sensitive relationship, especially with the principal. Line and staff relationship should be clear.
- Keeps the curriculum coordinator and/or principal informed so he/she can support the study.
- Attempts to keep up-to-date on the latest research and trends. He/she helps to locate resources and materials, may want to keep a file on community resources, and recommends material for the curriculum library. The librarian can be very helpful in locating and acquiring materials for curriculum studies. Lending support to the curriculum study should be a part of the librarian's work load; and released time from other duties should be provided, if needed.
- Serves as the public relations spokesman for this subject area and keeps others informed of the progress.

E. STUDY COMMITTEE CHAIRPERSON (AD HOC COMMITTEE)
THE CHAIRPERSON

- Should be a member of the subject area curriculum committee if there is one. First thing he/she should do is determine what his/her role is and get a job description, if possible. This may or may not be an administrator; probably not, unless it is a small school system.
- Guides the committee in carrying out its assignment. This is usually an "Ad Hoc" committee; that is, it is appointed for a specific task and then dissolved when the task is completed. Ad Hoc committees may be asked to identify the most urgent problems, study a specific problem, or review innovations for specific subject areas of the school curriculum.
- Prepares agendas and calls meetings.
- Keeps in close touch with building principals, curriculum coordinators, elementary and secondary directors, and teachers.
- Follows through, giving encouragement and recognition for work well done by committee members.

- Briefs others about the study as needed.
- Sees that the study keeps moving on schedule from day-to-day, mechanics of the study. This is where the problem is studied, and where the basic work is done.

F. TEACHER WHO IS A CURRICULUM COMMITTEE MEMBER

- Must consider new ideas as a challenge, not as a (threat) reflection on his/her past performance. Even more important, he/she must attempt to get other teachers to do the same.
- Tries to work as a group member and develop a cooperative spirit among all faculty, shows much interest and enthusiasm in the study.
- Is an advocate for the project, but does not overdo it. He/she interprets the committee's work to the faculty.
- Considers advice from consultants and others, and invites them to visit his/her classroom to observe experimentation if that is part of the study.
- Also may serve as a field-tester, writer, or as a participant in group discussions to help carry out the study.

G. TEACHER WHO IS NOT A CURRICULUM COMMITTEE MEMBER

- Should communicate his/her real concerns in writing to those on the committees. Is alert to an inadequate curriculum.
- Should participate in the curriculum study when appropriate, such as in planning and experimentation.
- Should evaluate his/her own program in terms of any new programs and not consider possible change as a personal threat. Teachers must be made to understand this.
- Should cooperate in both the experimentation and implementation of any new program; although probably not as enthusiastically as committee members.
- Knows and helps to identify student problems, feelings, and characteristics as they concern curriculum.
- (Since this individual will not be meeting formally, responsibilities should be communicated to him/her in writing. This correspondence should be done by the principal or curriculum coordinator, not the committee chairperson.)

H. CONSULTANT—IF ONE IS USED

- Learns as much as possible about the school district and its needs.
- Helps to clarify the task to be accomplished and who is to do it, including his/her own role.
- Specifies in writing what the consultant will do so everyone involved knows what is happening and when the task is completed.
- Works *with* the school personnel allowing solutions to problems to come from within if possible, however, does suggest alternatives when necessary.
- Keeps administrators informed, soliciting their help and cooperation at all times.
- Functions as a mediator or liaison when necessary as well as an expert, resource and

process person.
- Demonstrates how-to, not just telling how-to, if appropriate and applicable.
- Assists in locating materials and resources, including other resource personnel (consultants), if necessary.
- Helps to determine when the task is completed and summarizes it in writing, if appropriate and necessary.
- Helps to establish plans for follow-up activities, if appropriate and feasible.

Caution when using a consultant—both parties should agree on and preferably put in writing the following:

1. Definite purposes for the consultant's visits.
2. Define the areas in which the consultant will work.
3. Determine what is to be accomplished so all will know when the consultant is finished.
4. Set dates, times, and fee for consultant's visits.

Note: Those engaging the services of a consultant should specify what they want from a consultant and then ask for references of past work of this nature.

REFERENCES

Association for Supervision and Curriculum Development. *Curriculum Leaders: Improving Their Influence*. Washington, D.C.: Association for Supervision and Curriculum Development, 1976.

Clark, Leonard H.; Klein, Raymond L.; and Burks, John B. *The American Secondary School Curriculum* (2nd ed.). New York: Macmillan, 1972.

Doll, Ronald C. *Curriculum Improvement* (4th ed.). Boston: Allyn and Bacon, 1978.

Ford, Richard W. "How to Use a Consultant." *Educational Leadership*, November, 1972, 116-118.

Georgiades, William. "A Time To Do or Die, Curriculum Change: What Are The Ingredients?" *NASSP Bulletin*, March, 1980, *64*, 70-75.

Karmos, Joseph S. and Jacko, Carol M. "Innovations: A Note of Caution." *NASSP Bulletin*, October, 1977, 47-56.

Neagley, Ross L. and Evans, N. Dean. *Handbook for Effective Curriculum Development*. Englewood Cliffs, NJ: Prentice-Hall, 1967.

O'Hanlon, James and Wood, Fred H. "Regenerating the Curriculum Committee." *Educational Leadership*, November, 1972, *30*, 157-159.

Oliver, Albert I. *Curriculum Improvement: A Guide to Problems, Principles, and Process* (2nd ed.). New York: Harper and Row, 1977.

Ruff, Thomas P. "How to Use the Consultant." *Educational Leadership*, March 1974, 506-508.

Saylor, Galen J.; Alexander, William M.; and Lewis, Arthur J. *Curriculum Planning for Better Teaching and Learning* (4th ed.). Chicago: Holt, Rinehart and Winston, 1981.

Tankard, George C., Jr. *Curriculum Improvement: An Administrator's Guide*. West Nyack, NY: Parker, 1974.

Wiles, Jon and Bondi, Joseph, Jr. *Curriculum Development*. Columbus: Charles E. Merrill, 1979.

STEP VI

IDENTIFY AND ANALYZE POSSIBLE NEW CURRICULA, PROGRAMS, OR OTHER CURRICULAR INNOVATIONS TO MEET THE STATED CURRICULUM NEED

NOW THAT THE CURRICULAR NEED HAS BEEN ESTABLISHED, GOALS AND OBJECTIVES IDENTIFIED, REVISED, OR DEVELOPED, AND NECESSARY PRELIMINARY PREPARATION COMPLETED, IT IS TIME TO SEEK POSSIBLE SOLUTIONS TO THAT NEED. THIS WILL BE IN THE FORM OF NEW OR DIFFERENT CURRICULUM(A), PROGRAM(S), INNOVATION(S), OR PARTS OF THESE COMBINED TO MEET THE STATED CURRICULAR NEED. STEP VI WILL SERVE AS A GUIDE FOR IDENTIFYING AND ANALYZING POSSIBLE NEW CURRICULA, PROGRAMS, AND INNOVATIONS.

	CONSIDERING IT	PLANNING IT	DOING IT	COMPLETED	NOT NEEDED
VI. IDENTIFY AND ANALYZE POSSIBLE NEW CURRICULA, PROGRAMS, OR OTHER CURRICULAR INNOVATIONS TO MEET THE STATED CURRICULAR NEED					
A. IDENTIFY AND LOCATE SEVERAL NEW OR DIFFERENT CURRICULA, PROGRAMS, OR INNOVATIONS. GATHER INFORMATION BY:					
1. REVIEWING THE APPROPRIATE PROFESSIONAL, EDUCATIONAL, OR COMMERCIAL LITERATURE					
2. CONTACTING THE APPROPRIATE PROFESSIONAL, EDUCATIONAL, OR COMMERCIAL ASSOCIATION'S MAIN OFFICE —NATIONAL, STATE, AND LOCAL					
3. CONTACTING COLLEGES, UNIVERSITIES, AND NATIONAL, STATE, AND LOCAL DEPARTMENTS OF EDUCATION					
4. SEEKING THE ADVICE OF AUTHORITIES IN THE FIELD					
5. ATTENDING MEETINGS AND CONFERENCES RELATED TO THE CURRICULAR NEED					
6. VISITING SUCCESSFUL PROGRAMS IN OPERATION					
7. SEEKING INPUT FROM LOCAL PERSONNEL					
B. ANALYZE NEW CURRICULA OR PROGRAMS BY EXAMINING EACH FOR:					
1. PURPOSE—MAIN INTENT, GOALS OR OBJECTIVES					
2. ADVANTAGES AND DISADVANTAGES					
3. SUCCESSFUL APPROACHES, TECHNIQUES, AND IDEAS					
4. NECESSARY FACILITIES, EQUIPMENT, MATERIALS, AND RESOURCES					
5. COST—FOR PILOT AND/OR SYSTEM-WIDE IMPLEMENTATION					

STEP VI: EXPLANATION SECTION

VI.   **IDENTIFY AND ANALYZE POSSIBLE NEW CURRICULA, PROGRAMS, OR OTHER CURRICULAR INNOVATIONS FOR MEETING THE STATED CURRICULAR NEED**

A.   **IDENTIFY AND LOCATE SEVERAL NEW OR DIFFERENT CURRICULA, PROGRAMS, OR INNOVATIONS, AND GATHER INFORMATION ABOUT THEM. DO THIS BY:**

1.   **REVIEWING THE APPROPRIATE PROFESSIONAL, EDUCATIONAL, OR COMMERCIAL LITERATURE**

This information can usually be found in college and university libraries. Some school systems have professional or curriculum libraries where it can be located. The literature can sometimes be found and acquired from the source such as professional and educational association publishing offices. Information can also be acquired through commercial educational organizations as well as from businesses and industries by contacting their main headquarters or offices.

2.   **CONTACTING THE APPROPRIATE PROFESSIONAL, EDUCATIONAL, OR COMMERCIAL ASSOCIATION'S MAIN OFFICE—NATIONAL, STATE, AND LOCAL**

By contacting the main office of professional, educational or commercial associations, information relating to the subject being studied may be found. This is, at least, a starting point for identifying and locating what is available in the field. Through these offices, authorities and specialists in the field may also be located.

3.   **CONTACTING COLLEGES, UNIVERSITIES, AND NATIONAL, STATE, AND LOCAL DEPARTMENTS OF EDUCATION**

Colleges, universities, and departments of education at the national, state, and local levels are good sources for locating information, materials, and consultants in curricular fields.

4.   **SEEKING THE ADVICE OF AUTHORITIES IN THE FIELD**

Authorities or specialists in the subject being studied may be found in any of the previously mentioned sources as well as by attending meetings and conferences. It is a good idea to check on the specialists' work before accepting everything they are advocating, and ask for references of their work or where some of their ideas may be found in operation.

5.   **ATTENDING MEETINGS AND CONFERENCES RELATED TO THE CURRICULAR NEED**

Information, materials, and specialists in the field can be located at meetings, conferences, or workshops pertaining to the curricular topic being studied.

6. VISITING SUCCESSFUL PROGRAMS IN OPERATION

One of the best ways to determine what a new curriculum or program will do is to observe it at work. Before visits are made to observe a new program in operation, the program should be studied in depth. Some specific things to look for and ask about should be established prior to the visitation.

7. SEEKING INPUT FROM LOCAL PERSONNEL

It is possible that individuals from within the school system have as much expertise on the topic being studied as some of those who claim to be authorities. If this is the case, those persons, by all means, should be utilized to the fullest extent. They could be responsible for certain steps of the study, or perhaps, even placed in charge of the entire planning, studying, and development of the topic.

B. ANALYZE NEW CURRICULA OR PROGRAMS BY EXAMINING EACH FOR:
1. PURPOSE—MAIN INTENT, GOALS OR OBJECTIVES

The planner should seek any goals and/or objectives that are stated for the new programs. These goals and objectives should be compared with the school system's goals to determine if they fulfill or contribute to them in any way. This comparison of goals also helps to determine if the new program will meet the curricular need being studied. Getting more specific, some of the following questions should be asked: Will this change make a positive contribution to the growth and development of the students? Can the change operate successfully in this school system? Have other systems made this change successfully? If so, were their constraints similar to those in this school system?

2. ADVANTAGES AND DISADVANTAGES

Just as there are two sides to any story, there are two sides to any curriculum or program. By making a list of advantages and a list of disadvantages of each program being studied, especially as it is related to the stated curricular need, a comparison can be made as to what it will do to meet that need.

3. SUCCESSFUL APPROACHES, TECHNIQUES, AND IDEAS

Everything possible about the new program should be studied. Especially helpful are individuals who have used the program; if possible, their likes and dislikes, suggestions, hints, and helps regarding the program should be obtained.

4. NECESSARY FACILITIES, EQUIPMENT, MATERIALS, AND RESOURCES

While examining the new programs, it is advisable to make a list of the major facilities, equipment, or materials which will be needed to implement each program. Later in this process these items for each new program will be compared with what the school system has or can procure.

5. **COST FOR PILOT AND/OR ADOPTION SYSTEM-WIDE IMPLEMENTATION**
    It is important to obtain all the information possible about the cost of each new program. If the innovation is to be tried on a limited (pilot) basis first, an attempt should be made to gather information that would help estimate that as well as for implementing the new program system-wide. Information about cost should be collected for each program even if it is only a rough estimation.

REFERENCES

Bushnell, David S. "A Systematic Strategy for School Renewal." *Educational Technology*, February, 1972, 27-33.

Doll, Ronald C. *Curriculum Improvement* (4th ed.). Boston: Allyn and Bacon, 1978.

Neagley, Ross L. and Evans, N. Dean. *Handbook for Effective Curriculum Development*. Englewood Cliffs, NJ: Prentice-Hall, 1967.

Pratt, David. *Curriculum, Design and Development*. New York: Harcourt Brace Jovanovich, 1980.

Saylor, Galen J.; Alexander, William M.; and Lewis, Arthur J. *Curriculum Planning for Better Teaching and Learning* (4th ed.). Chicago: Holt, Rinehart and Winston, 1981.

STEP VII

ASSESS AND SELECT ONE OF THE NEW CURRICULA, PROGRAMS, OR OTHER

CURRICULAR INNOVATIONS TO MEET THE STATED CURRICULAR NEED

NOW THAT POSSIBLE NEW CURRICULA, PROGRAMS, OR OTHER CURRICULAR INNO-VATIONS HAVE BEEN IDENTIFIED AND ANALYZED, EACH OF THEM SHOULD BE ASSESSED IN TERMS OF THE STATED CURRICULAR NEED. ONE (OR A COMBINATION OF SEVERAL) PROGRAM(S) SHOULD THEN BE SELECTED AND TRIED (ON A PILOT BASIS FIRST) TO MEET THAT STATED NEED.

	CONSIDERING IT	PLANNING IT	DOING IT	COMPLETED	NOT NEEDED
VII. ASSESS AND SELECT ONE OF THE NEW CURRICULA, PROGRAMS, OR OTHER CURRICULUM INNOVATIONS TO MEET THE STATED CURRICULAR NEED					
A. ASSESS EACH POSSIBLE NEW CURRICULUM OR PROGRAM					
1. DESCRIBE HOW IT WILL MEET THE STATED CURRICULUM NEED					
2. DESCRIBE HOW IT WILL CONTRIBUTE TO THE GOALS OF THE SCHOOL SYSTEM					
3. DESCRIBE HOW IT WILL FIT INTO AND WORK IN THIS PARTICULAR SCHOOL SYSTEM IN TERMS OF:					
a. STAFF					
b. STUDENTS					
c. COMMUNITY					
d. FACILITIES					
e. EQUIPMENT					
f. RESOURCES AND MATERIALS					
g. COST					
B. SELECT ONE NEW CURRICULUM OR PROGRAM					
1. SELECT THE ONE NEW CURRICULUM OR PROGRAM (OR A COMBINATION OF SEVERAL) THAT SEEMS TO BEST MEET THE STATED CURRICULAR NEED AND FIT INTO THE SCHOOL SYSTEM					
2. LIST THE REASONS WHY THIS SELECTED CURRICULUM OR PROGRAM SHOULD BE TRIED INCLUDING HOW IT WILL CONTRIBUTE TO THE STATED CURRICULAR NEED AND SCHOOL SYSTEM GOALS					

STEP VII: EXPLANATION SECTION

VII. ASSESS AND SELECT ONE OF THE NEW CURRICULA, PROGRAMS, OR OTHER CURRICULAR INNOVATIONS TO MEET THE STATED CURRICULAR NEED

A. ASSESS EACH POSSIBLE NEW CURRICULUM OR PROGRAM

1. DESCRIBE HOW IT WILL MEET THE STATED CURRICULAR NEED

The planner should describe how each new program's purpose and goals found in Step VI would fulfill or contribute in some way to the curricular stated need in Step I. Checking the advantages and disadvantages of each new program may also assist in determining if that program would contribute to the need. By writing this out for each new program, a comparison can be made and the one identified that is best designed to meet the curricular need.

2. DESCRIBE HOW IT WILL CONTRIBUTE TO GOALS OF THE SCHOOL SYSTEM

Curriculum planners should describe how each new program's purpose and goals found in Step VI would fulfill or contribute in some way to the school's district-wide goals. The district goals were either already established or developed in Step II. One way to visually show how many of each new program's goals contribute to the school system's goals is to place them in columns and match them like a set of matching test items. The new program with the most goals matching those of the school district should be the one that would contribute most to the school curricula.

3. DESCRIBE HOW IT WILL FIT INTO AND WORK IN THIS PARTICULAR SCHOOL SYSTEM IN TERMS OF:

- STAFF.
- STUDENTS.
- COMMUNITY.
- FACILITIES.
- EQUIPMENT.
- RESOURCES AND MATERIALS.
- COST.
- OTHER _____.

All of these seem to be self-explanatory. Simply stated, does the school system have the staff, facilities, equipment, resources, and materials to implement the new program? Also, will the students and community accept the new curriculum? And, is there sufficient money available to cover making these changes?

B. **SELECT ONE NEW CURRICULUM OR PROGRAM**

   1. **SELECT THE ONE NEW CURRICULUM OR PROGRAM (OR COMBINATION OF SEVERAL) THAT SEEMS TO BEST MEET THE STATED CURRICULAR NEED AND FIT INTO THE SCHOOL SYSTEM**

      Using the analysis information from Step VI and the assessment information from (Substep A) of this Step, the one curriculum, program, or combination of several, that has the most items fitting the need and goals of this particular school system can be identified and selected. If it is a packaged program, it will probably need to be redesigned to fit the system. If it is a whole new concept being developed into a program, it will probably need to be completely designed to fit the present school setting. Whichever the case, Step VIII, Curriculum Design, of this Handbook will serve as a guide to do it. The new program is then ready to be implemented (Step IX) on a pilot basis first, and evaluated (Step X) to determine if it should be adopted as part of the permanent curriculum.

   2. **LIST THE REASONS WHY THIS SELECTED NEW PROGRAM SHOULD BE TRIED, INCLUDING HOW IT WILL CONTRIBUTE TO THE STATED CURRICULAR NEED AND GOALS OF THE SCHOOL SYSTEM**

      This is the point at which the new program is presented to the decision makers for acceptance. When everything is listed that the program is designed to accomplish, the best possible case can be made for trying it. The goals of the program should be listed and an explanation given as to how they will contribute to and help fulfill the goals of the school system. The planners should explain that this curricular need, and possible new programs to meet that need, have been studied for the past one, one and one-half, or two years. Based on that study, the new program should help students to make certain achievements. These accomplishments should be listed and described. If the curriculum planners do a thorough job of organizing and presenting the new program as just described, the chances of its acceptance by the decision makers are very good, unless the cost is entirely beyond reason.

REFERENCES

Bushnell, David S. "A Systematic Strategy for School Renewal." *Educational Technology*, February, 1972, 27-33.

Doll, Ronald C. *Curriculum Improvement* (4th ed.). Boston: Allyn and Bacon, 1978.

Findley, Dale and Hamm, Russell. "The Bandwagon Approach to Curricular Innovation: Look Before You Leap." *NASSP Bulletin*, October, 1977, *61*, 57-60.

Hunkins, Francis P. *Curriculum Development: Program Improvement*. Columbus: Charles E. Merrill, 1980.

Neagley, Ross L. and Evans, N. Dean. *Handbook for Effective Curriculum Development*. Englewood Cliffs, NJ: Prentice-Hall, 1967.

Pratt, David. *Curriculum, Design and Development*. New York: Harcourt Brace Jovanovich, 1980.

Saylor, Galen J.; Alexander, William M.; and Lewis, Arthur J. *Curriculum Planning for Better Teaching and Learning* (4th ed.). Chicago: Holt, Rinehart and Winston, 1981.

Wiles, Jon and Bondi, Joseph, Jr. *Curriculum Development*. Columbus: Charles E. Merrill, 1979.

Zahorik, John A. "Learning Activities: The Objectives—Seeking Function." *The Elementary School Journal*, September, 1976, *77*, 50-56.

STEP VIII

DESIGN OR REDESIGN THE NEW CURRICULUM OR PROGRAM

(CURRICULUM DESIGN)

ONCE A NEW CURRICULUM, PROGRAM, OR CHANGES TO THE PRESENT CURRICULUM HAVE BEEN SELECTED, THE NEXT STEP IS TO DESIGN OR REDESIGN IT TO FIT THE EXISTING SCHOOL SETTING. IF A WHOLE NEW PROGRAM IS TO BE DEVELOPED, IT WILL HAVE TO BE COMPLETELY DESIGNED. IF A PACKAGED PROGRAM IS SELECTED, IT WILL HAVE TO BE REDESIGNED TO FIT THE PRESENT SCHOOL SYSTEM. THIS STEP IS A GUIDE FOR DOING BOTH.

	CONSIDERING IT	PLANNING IT	DOING IT	COMPLETED	NOT NEEDED
VIII. DESIGN OR REDESIGN THE NEW CURRICULUM OR PROGRAM (CURRICULUM DESIGN)					
A. SELECT LEARNING OPPORTUNITY (DESIGN) TO BE USED IN THE NEW PROGRAM					
B. IDENTIFY THE MAJOR AREAS OF KNOWLEDGE, CONCEPTS, TOPICS, SKILLS, AND CONTENT TO BE INCLUDED IN THE NEW PROGRAM. THESE COULD BE STATED IN THE FORM OF GOALS					
C. IDENTIFY AND DETERMINE AVAILABILITY OF FACILITIES, STAFF, MATERIALS, EQUIPMENT, FUNDS, AND ANY OTHER RESOURCES REQUIRED FOR IMPLEMENTATION OF THE NEW PROGRAM					
D. DETERMINE IF AND HOW THE NEW PROGRAM WILL FIT INTO THE SCHOOL SYSTEM'S SCHEDULE					
(USE THIS CHECKLIST IF DESIGNING A COURSE)					
A. DEVELOP THE MAIN PURPOSE OF THE COURSE. THIS CAN BE CALLED PHILOSOPHY OF THE COURSE					
B. ESTABLISH THE COURSE GOALS. THIS INCLUDES THE MAJOR AREAS OF KNOWLEDGE, CONCEPTS, TOPICS, SKILLS, AND CONTENT TO BE COVERED IN THE COURSE. (TEXTBOOKS COULD BE SELECTED AT THIS POINT; HOWEVER, IT IS RECOMMENDED THAT THEY BE SELECTED DURING THE NEXT STEP, IMPLEMENTATION.)					
C. DEVELOP COURSE TERMINAL BEHAVIORAL OBJECTIVES (WHAT THE PARTICIPANTS SHOULD BE ABLE TO DO AFTER COMPLETING THE COURSE)					
D. IDENTIFY AND DETERMINE AVAILABILITY OF ALL MATERIALS AND EQUIPMENT THAT ARE NECESSARY TO TEACH (IMPLEMENT) THE COURSE					
E. DEVELOP A COURSE OF STUDY OR SOME TYPE OF COURSE OUTLINE TO GUIDE INSTRUCTION (IMPLEMENTATION) OF THE COURSE					

VIII. DESIGN OR REDESIGN THE NEW CURRICULUM OR PROGRAM (CURRICULUM DESIGN)

A. SELECT LEARNING OPPORTUNITY (DESIGN) TO BE USED IN THE NEW PROGRAM

The curriculum or program design as used here is the organization and arrangement of learning opportunities for students. Learning opportunities may be any plan, subjects, or courses that provide a way to organize the opportunity for students to learn. Some of the most common types of learning opportunities are:

- Subjects
- Courses
- Mini-Courses
- Workshops
- Independent Studies
- Tutorial Sessions
- On-the-job Training

The learning opportunities (design) should be arranged so as to provide balance and articulation (vertical and horizontal) in the school system curriculum. This can be done the same way as described in Step I of this Handbook, pages 10-12.

Once the new curriculum or program has been selected and the goals of that program established, the next step is to design it into subjects, courses, mini-courses, or what seems most appropriate and also fits into the school system. The curricular need that is to be met should be kept in mind as the new program or course is being designed.

B. IDENTIFY MAJOR AREAS OF KNOWLEDGE, CONCEPTS, TOPICS, SKILLS AND CONTENT TO BE INCLUDED IN THE NEW PROGRAM. THESE CAN BE STATED IN THE FORM OF GOALS

Now that the goals and learning opportunities of the new program have been established, the major areas of knowledge, concepts, topics, skills, and subject matter content to be included should be identified. This is sometimes done in the form of broadly stated general objectives or goals. Whichever way is used, an outline of the major content to be included is specified. Two important points at this stage should be noted. First, the content is identified, not necessarily selected; and secondly, the content is stated in broad terms. The actual selection of the subject matter content, scope and sequence, and the development of specific behavioral objectives is to be done by the teacher during the implementation stage. If it is a course that is being designed, the writing of behavioral objectives and the selection of content as well as textbooks can be done at this stage.

C. IDENTIFY AND DETERMINE AVAILABILITY OF FACILITIES, STAFF, MATERIALS, EQUIPMENT, FUNDS, AND ANY OTHER RESOURCES REQUIRED FOR IMPLEMENTATION OF THE NEW PROGRAM

This is the point at which the actual identification and determination is made of what is needed, and if it is or can be made available for the instructional phase. This refers to staff, facilities, equipment, materials, or funds required to implement the program. If there is anything that cannot be acquired, then (Substep B) of this Step should be rechecked to see if something that was identified to be covered has to be deleted. It should be noted here at the Design phase that these things are identified as being available. They are not actually obtained for use until the next Step, Implementation.

D. DETERMINE IF AND HOW THE NEW PROGRAM WILL FIT INTO THE SCHOOL SYSTEM'S SCHEDULE

The new program may be very acceptable to this point, but it now must be determined if the program will fit into the present schedule of classes and activities of the school. Will other parts of the curriculum have to be changed or altered because of this program? Simply stated, can it be worked into the way things are currently being done? If not, then the next Step (Implementation) should not be attempted.

COURSE DESIGN OR DEVELOPMENT

SINCE A COURSE IS THE MOST COMMONLY USED CURRICULUM DESIGN, AN OUTLINE FOR DEVELOPING A COURSE FOLLOWS AS AN EXAMPLE:

A. DEVELOP THE MAIN PURPOSE OF THE COURSE. THIS CAN BE CALLED A PHILOSOPHY OF THE COURSE.

The first thing that should be established when designing a course is the main purpose or rationale for it. The planner should state what the course is designed to do and why that is important. This may or may not be called a philosophy and is usually included in the introduction to the course. What it is called is not as important as making sure that the main purpose is clear before developing the course.

B. ESTABLISH THE COURSE GOALS. THIS INCLUDES THE MAJOR AREAS OF KNOWLEDGE, CONCEPTS, TOPICS, SKILLS, AND CONTENT TO BE COVERED IN THE COURSE. (TEXTBOOKS COULD BE SELECTED AT THIS POINT; HOWEVER, IT IS RECOMMENDED THAT THEY BE SELECTED DURING THE NEXT STEP, IMPLEMENTATION.)

At this stage, the planners should decide which broad major content areas are to be included in the course. These are sometimes called goals or general objectives. Whatever they are called, they are the general broad concepts to be presented. At this point, no reference needs to be made as to how the information will be taught or learned, merely what is to be included in the course. Also at this stage, the course is only being designed and not taught. Therefore, the selection of the actual content and textbook is probably not done; those decisions come in the next Step which is Implementation. Some consideration should be given here, however, to the approximate time allotment of major areas, so as not to identify more than can reasonably be handled in such a course. If the course is going to be taught by the same individual(s) who designs it, then the textbook and scope and sequence of the content can be selected at this stage.

C. **DEVELOP COURSE TERMINAL BEHAVIORAL OBJECTIVES (WHAT THE PARTICIPANTS SHOULD BE ABLE TO DO AFTER COMPLETING THE COURSE)**

Course terminal objectives refer to the broad, yet specific, things that participants should be able to do after completing the course. These are not the daily behavioral objectives of each lesson, but instead, a consolidation of those daily objectives into a broader statement. A chapter or unit will usually have 8, 10, or 12 specific behavioral objectives which can be consolidated into one or two terminal objectives. (See Step II, pages 21-25, for an example.) A course then usually finishes with 8, 10, 12, or possibly 15, broad course terminal objectives which can be managed much easier than the 80, 100 or more daily student behavioral objectives. Fewer broad terminal objectives make it easier to guide and evaluate the course.

To develop these objectives, one of two procedures can be used. First, the objectives can be established before teaching the course and then revised as the course is taught. Secondly, if there is not sufficient time to develop objectives before the course begins, the major items can be written out as they are covered each day and then rewritten so that the information is in the form of student behavioral objectives at the end of each week. At the end of each chapter or unit, the teacher can then consolidate these student behavioral objectives into course terminal objectives. Developing objectives as the course is taught may not be the best way to proceed. However, it may be the only way a teacher can develop them at this time; and that is better than not writing them at all.

D. **IDENTIFY AND DETERMINE AVAILABILITY OF ALL MATERIALS AND EQUIPMENT THAT ARE NECESSARY TO TEACH (IMPLEMENT) THE COURSE**

Now the facilities, equipment, materials and funds should be listed that will be needed to teach the course. Then those that are already available should be checked. Next, those items that are listed as needed but not readily accessible should be approved by the individual who has the authority to decide if they can be acquired. If it is impossible to obtain any of these, then the major concepts, topics and skills to be covered and objectives to be achieved may have to be changed. This is the time to determine what can and cannot be acquired; planners should not wait until the next phase, Implementation, (instruction). This means the course needs to be designed well in advance of its implementation.

E. **DEVELOP A COURSE OF STUDY OR SOME TYPE OF COURSE OUTLINE TO GUIDE INSTRUCTION (IMPLEMENTATION) OF THE COURSE**

The curriculum plans which have been established to this point should be put into writing. A full-fledged curriculum guide may not be desirable or even possible at this stage, but some type of rough outline or course of study should be developed to guide implementation of the new plans. (See Appendix A for writing curriculum guides.) Written guides help those who are designing the course, as well as those who are responsible for supervising it, to know what is happening. Teaching units could be developed at this stage; however, they probably would not be done until the next Step which is Implementation. Teaching units are described in Step IX, Implementation, of the Handbook.

REFERENCES

Alexander, Lawrence T. and Yelon, Stephen L. "The Use of a Common Experiential Referent in Instructional System Design." *Educational Technology*, April, 1969, *9*, 44-46.

Bulach, Cletus R. "An Organizational Plan for Curriculum Development." *Educational Leadership*, January, 1978, *35*, 308-312.

Callahan, Joseph F. and Clark, Leonard H. *Teaching in the Secondary School*. New York: Macmillan, 1977.

Corwin, Rebecca; Hein, George E.; and Levin, Diane. "Weaving Curriculum Webs: The Structure of Nonlinear Curriculum." *Childhood Education*, March, 1976, *52*, 248-251.

Doll, Ronald C. *Curriculum Improvement* (4th ed.). Boston: Allyn and Bacon, 1978.

Feldhusen, John F.; Ames, Russel E., Jr.; and Linden, Kathryn W. "Designing Instruction to Achieve Higher Level Goals and Objectives." *Educational Technology*, October, 1974, *14*, 21-23.

Glatthorn, Allan A. *Alternatives in Education: Schools and Programs*. New York: Dodd, Mead, 1975.

Hauenstein, A. Dean. *Curriculum Planning for Behavioral Development*. Worthington, OH: Charles A. Jones, 1972.

Hunkins, Francis P. *Curriculum Development: Program Improvement*. Columbus: Charles E. Merrill, 1980.

Johnston, A. Montgomery. "The Open Curriculum: A Definition." *Tennessee Education*, Winter, 1977, *6*, 23-27.

Karmos, Joseph S. and Jacko, Carol M. "Innovations: A Note of Caution." *NASSP Bulletin*, October, 1977, 47-56.

Lewy, Arieh. *Planning the School Curriculum*. Paris: Unesco, International Institute for Educational Planning, 1977.

Neagley, Ross L. and Evans, N. Dean. *Handbook for Effective Curriculum Development*. Englewood

69

Cliffs, NJ: Prentice-Hall, 1967.

Pratt, David. *Curriculum, Design and Development*. New York: Harcourt Brace Jovanovich, 1980.

Saylor, Galen J.; Alexander, William M.; and Lewis, Arthur J. *Curriculum Planning for Better Teaching and Learning* (4th ed.). Chicago: Holt, Rinehart and Winston, 1981.

Tankard, George C., Jr. *Curriculum Improvement: An Administrator's Guide*. West Nyack, NY: Parker, 1974.

Thompson, Donald L. and Borsari, Leonard R. "An Overview of Management by Objectives for Guidance and Counseling Services." *The School Counselor* June, 1978, *25*, 172-177.

Tyler, Ralph W. "Specific Approaches to Curriculum Development." In James R. Gress and David E. Purpel (Eds.), *Curriculum, An Introduction to the Field*. Berkeley: McCutchan, 1978.

Wiles, Jon and Bondi, Joseph, Jr. *Curriculum Development*. Columbus: Charles E. Merrill, 1979.

Williams, William H. "Major Steps in Developing Curriculum." *Industrial Education*, September, 1971, *60*, 79-81.

STEP IX

IMPLEMENT THE NEW CURRICULUM OR PROGRAM (CURRICULUM IMPLEMENTATION)

ONCE THE NEW CURRICULUM OR PROGRAM HAS BEEN DESIGNED OR REDESIGNED TO FIT A GIVEN SCHOOL SYSTEM, THE NEXT STEP IS TO IMPLEMENT OR PUT IT INTO OPERATION. THERE ARE, HOWEVER, SEVERAL PRELIMINARY TASKS TO BE COMPLETED BEFORE A NEW PROGRAM CAN BEGIN. THIS STEP SERVES AS A GUIDE FOR PERFORMING THOSE TASKS.

IX. IMPLEMENT THE NEW CURRICULUM OR PROGRAM (CURRICULUM IMPLEMENTATION)

	CONSIDERING IT	PLANNING IT	DOING IT	COMPLETED	NOT NEEDED
A. DESIGNATE ONE INDIVIDUAL TO BE IN CHARGE OF IMPLE-MENTING THE NEW CURRICULUM OR PROGRAM					
B. OBTAIN ALL NECESSARY CLEARANCES (INCLUDING FUNDS, FACILITIES, AND EQUIPMENT)					
C. SELECT STAFF AND ORIENT THEM (TRAIN IF NECESSARY) TO THE NEW PROGRAM, SUBJECT, OR COURSE					
D. SELECT AND PREPARE THE ACTUAL SITE AND FACILITIES TO BE USED					
E. SET THE TIME AND SCHEDULE TO BE USED					
F. INSTRUCTORS SELECT AND ORGANIZE THE SUBJECT MATTER CONTENT TO BE USED (INCLUDING THE SELECTION OF TEXT-BOOKS AND RELATED MATERIAL)					
G. INSTRUCTORS MAKE CERTAIN ALL EQUIPMENT, MATERIALS, AND OTHER RESOURCES NEEDED ARE READY TO USE					
H. INSTRUCTORS PREPARE THE INSTRUCTIONAL PLAN OR TEACHING UNIT					
I. ASSESS THE NEW PROGRAM AS IT PROGRESSES (FORMATIVE EVALUATION)					

IX. **IMPLEMENT THE NEW CURRICULUM OR PROGRAM (CURRICULUM IMPLEMENTATION)**

A. **DESIGNATE ONE INDIVIDUAL TO BE IN CHARGE OF IMPLEMENTING THE NEW CURRICULUM OR PROGRAM**

Now that the new program is going to be put into operation, one individual has to be in charge to guide and monitor the action. Someone has to say, "We begin now; yes, we do this; no, we do not do that." This person's task is to keep the project moving and to bring it to a close when the plan is complete. It is very important that the person in charge has the *authority* to make decisions when necessary. There are times, of course, that he/she may have to contact higher authorities before making a decision. But the main point here is that someone is in charge and responsible for keeping the new program going.

B. **OBTAIN ALL NECESSARY CLEARANCES (INCLUDING FUNDS, FACILITIES, AND EQUIPMENT)**

One of the first duties of the individual in charge of implementation is to make certain any clearances or approvals needed are received. This includes funds that are used and final arrangements to be made concerning facilities, equipment, materials, and any other resources required to begin instruction.

C. **SELECT STAFF AND ORIENT THEM (TRAIN IF NECESSARY) TO THE NEW PROGRAM, SUBJECT, OR COURSE**

Before the action can begin, someone has to be chosen to do it. Since we are dealing with educational curricula or programs here, we are usually referring to an instructional staff of some type. Therefore, the staff has to be chosen and prepared. The type of program will determine whether the staff simply needs to be reoriented or if they will need to be completely reeducated or retrained. Those who are going to be teaching the new program will need adequate time to understand the materials and prepare themselves to teach it. This is a very *important* step that is often overlooked or neglected by those who are in charge of the implementation process, which may be one of the reasons why teachers sometimes resist change and new curricula.

If a guide of some type for the new program has not been developed by now, it could be done at this point. It would need to be a looseleaf curriculum guide because after the new program has been implemented, usually there are some changes needed. A looseleaf guide permits pages to be added and removed as necessary. (See Appendix A for instructions to develop curriculum guides.)

D. **SELECT AND PREPARE THE ACTUAL SITE AND FACILITIES TO BE USED**

At this point the actual site and facilities have to be prepared for use. The individual in charge of implementation must specify the buildings, classrooms, or whatever is required, and prepare them to be used for this particular program or course.

E. SET THE TIME AND SCHEDULE TO BE USED

There is no exact order that these, as well as some of the other items in this Step, are to be done. Some may have been completed during the design stage. However, before the new program can move into operation, certain matters have to be determined and readied. Setting the exact time and schedule of the new program do have to be specified for the implementation stage to begin.

F. INSTRUCTORS SELECT AND ORGANIZE THE SUBJECT MATTER CONTENT TO BE USED (INCLUDING THE SELECTION OF TEXTBOOKS AND RELATED MATERIAL)

This is the place where those who are responsible for the actual teaching of the program are to select the subject matter content to be taught. In school systems, this primarily would be classroom teachers.

The selection of the subject matter content, for the most part, means the selection of textbooks and is an extremely important part of instruction. Research from EPIE (1977) indicates that 95 percent of the students' time spent in school classrooms is centered around the textbook. Therefore, selecting textbooks is a very important part of the implementation process of any instructional program. (See Appendix B for a guide to evaluating and selecting textbooks.) Once the textbook and other instructional material have been selected for the new program, teachers definitely should be given adequate time to study the materials and prepare themselves to teach it.

G. INSTRUCTORS MAKE CERTAIN ALL EQUIPMENT, MATERIALS, AND OTHER RESOURCES NEEDED ARE READY TO USE

In the Design stage, equipment, materials, and other resources were identified as being available; now is the time to obtain them and make certain they are ready to use. Resources may include community resources, such as guest speakers and sites to visit, which cannot be collected but can be listed and scheduled into the instructional timetable.

H. INSTRUCTORS PREPARE THE INSTRUCTIONAL PLAN OR TEACHING UNIT

Implementation almost always means instruction or teaching of some type. It is the teacher who is responsible for the instructional or teaching unit. Instructional units vary in format and organization however, most of them are developed by the teacher at the time of instruction and will include the following basic information.
1. Approximate time that will be needed to complete the unit.
2. Subject matter content to be taught. This is usually an outline of the main topics to be covered.
3. Objectives to be achieved. These are usually written in specific or behavioral terms. This is what the students will be able to do at the end of instruction.
4. Procedures and activities to be used to accomplish these objectives. This includes the teaching strategies used by the teacher and the learning activities in which students will participate.
5. Materials and resources that will be used.

6. Assessment procedures that will be used to determine the degree to which the objectives were accomplished. The methods used to determine the amount of achievement by the students is the responsibility of the instructor. Pre-posttesting could be used.

Even if it is something other than teaching units involved, the same type of organization and information outlined in these six steps could be useful as a guide for implementation. (See Appendix C for an example of a teaching unit.)

I. **ASSESS THE NEW PROGRAM AS IT PROGRESSES (FORMATIVE EVALUATION)**

This phase is probably completed by the group or individual who is in charge of curriculum development in the school system. It could be done by the instructors of the new program, although probably not, except for the part where they are directly involved.

Formative evaluation includes keeping a written account of the program's development beginning with the planning stage. This record of events helps to compare actual progress with the planned progress and to make minor adjustments in the program as it proceeds. It also helps as a point of reference for summative (total) evaluation at the completion of the implementation stage.

Those responsibile for curriculum development should keep everyone who is involved in any way, directly or indirectly, informed of the new program's progress. They, in some way, should reward those who are directly involved in the program. Money could be used as a reward; however, it may not be permissible or necessarily the best reward. Praise is often very effective, especially if it comes from authority figures, such as the superintendent, curriculum coordinator, or principal of the school.

REFERENCES

A Model for Selecting Instructional Materials. Stony Brook, NY: Educational Products Information Exchange Institute (EPIE Institute), 1979.

Beauchamp, George A. "A Hard Look at Curriculum." *Educational Leadership*, February, 1978, *35*, 404-409.

Bell, Chip R. "Criteria for Selecting Instructional Strategies." *Training and Development Journal*, October, 1977, *31*, 3-7.

Bulach, Cletus R. "An Organizational Plan for Curriculum Development." *Educational Leadership*, January, 1978, *35*, 308-312.

Doll, Ronald C. *Curriculum Development* (4th ed.). Boston: Allyn and Bacon, 1978.

Feldhusen, John F.; Ames, Russel E., Jr.; and Linden, Kathryn W. "Designing Instruction to Achieve Higher Level Goals and Objectives." *Educational Technology*, October, 1974, *14*, 21-23.

Frey, William Paul. "How to Keep Those New Programs Alive and Well." *Educational Leadership*, December, 1979, *37*, 208-210.

Gottesman, Alexander M. "Applying a Model in Curriculum Planning." *NASSP Bulletin*, September, 1977, *61*, 24-30.

Hauenstein, A. Dean. *Curriculum Planning for Behavioral Development*. Worthington, OH: Charles A. Jones, 1972.

Hunkins, Francis P. *Curriculum Development: Program Improvement*. Columbus: Charles E. Merrill, 1980.

Jordan, Lucille G. "Systematizing Curricular Planning and Implementation: What a Supervisor Can Do." *Educational Leadership*, October, 1978, *36*, 41-45.

Kim, Eugene C. and Kellough, Richard D. *A Resource Guide for Secondary School Teaching* (2nd ed.). New York: Macmillan, 1978.

Neagley, Ross L. and Evans, N. Dean. *Handbook for Effective Curriculum Development*. Englewood Cliffs, NJ: Prentice-Hall, 1967.

Nolan, John. "The Use and Misuse of Films in Management Training." *Training and Development Journal*, March, 1980, 84-86.

Oliver, Albert I. *Curriculum Improvement: A Guide to Problems, Principles, and Process* (2nd ed.). New York: Harper and Row, 1977.

Palmatier, Larry L. "How Teachers Can Innovate and Still Keep Their Jobs." *Journal of Teacher Education*, Spring, 1975, *26*, 60-62.

Patterson, Jerry L. and Czajkowski, Theodore J. "Implementation: Neglected Phase in Curriculum Change." *Educational Leadership*, December, 1979, *37*, 204-206.

Pratt, David. *Curriculum, Design and Development*. New York: Harcourt Brace Jovanovich, 1980.

Rooze, Gene E. "Planning for Curriculum Implementation: A New Perspective." *Educational Technology*, July, 1971, *11*, 58-60.

Saylor, Galen J.; Alexander, William M.; and Lewis, Arthur J. *Curriculum Planning for Better Teaching and Learning* (4th ed.). Chicago: Holt, Rinehart and Winston, 1981.

Tankard, George C., Jr. *Curriculum Improvement: An Administrator's Guide.* West Nyack, NY: Parker, 1974.

Thoms, Denis F. "Implementing the Curriculum/Program." *Educational Technology*, July, 1978, *18*, 5-9.

Tyler, Ralph W. "Specific Approaches to Curriculum Development." In James R. Gress and David E. Purpel (Eds.), *Curriculum, An Introduction to the Field*. Berkeley: McCutchan, 1978.

Wasserman, Selma. "Teachers and Curriculum Makers." *Childhood Education*, March, 1976, *52*, 242-247.

Wickert, Jack J. "Criteria for Curriculum Development." *Educational Leadership*, January, 1973, *30*, 339-342.

Wiles, Jon and Bondi, Joseph, Jr. *Curriculum Development*. Columbus: Charles E. Merrill, 1979.

Williams, William H. "Major Steps in Developing Curriculum." *Industrial Education*, September, 1971, *60*, 79-81.

Zahorik, John A. "Learning Activities: The Objectives-Seeking Function." *The Elementary School Journal*, 1976, *77*, 50-56.

Zenger, Sharon K. and Zenger, Weldon F. *57 Ways To Teach*. Los Angeles: Crescent, 1977.

STEP X

EVALUATE THE NEW CURRICULUM OR PROGRAM (CURRICULUM EVALUATION)

CURRICULUM EVALUATION IS A CONTINUOUS PROCESS AND SHOULD BE AT THE BE-GINNING, THROUGHOUT, AND AT THE COMPLETION OF CURRICULUM DEVELOPMENT. EVALUATING CURRICULUM STUDIES FROM THE BEGINNING AND AS THEY PROGRESS IS FORMATIVE EVALUATION AND WAS PRESENTED AS THE LAST PART OF STEP IX IN THIS HANDBOOK. STEP X SERVES AS A GUIDE FOR SUMMATIVE EVALUATION, WHICH IS TO EVALUATE CURRICULA AS IT EXISTS OR UPON COMPLETION OF CURRICULUM DEVELOP-MENT.

X. **EVALUATE THE NEW CURRICULUM OR PROGRAM (CURRICULUM EVALUATION)**

	CONSIDERING IT	PLANNING IT	DOING IT	COMPLETED	NOT NEEDED
A. SPECIFY WHAT IS TO BE EVALUATED—ENTIRE CURRICULUM, SPECIFIC PROGRAM, OR A SPECIFIC SUBJECT AREA, AND FOR WHAT PURPOSE—CONTENT COORDINATION, CONTENT ACHIEVEMENT, ETC.					
B. DETERMINE CRITERIA TO BE USED TO MAKE THE EVALUATION					
C. IDENTIFY INFORMATION (DATA) NEEDED FOR THE EVALUATION					
D. DECIDE HOW TO COLLECT NEEDED INFORMATION (DATA) FOR THE EVALUATION					
E. COLLECT AND ANALYZE INFORMATION (DATA) FOR THE EVALUATION					
F. EVALUATE INFORMATION (DATA) AND MAKE DECISIONS					

X. **EVALUATE THE NEW CURRICULUM OR PROGRAM (CURRICULUM EVALUATION)**

Evaluation, though probably the most important phase of curriculum planning and development, is often either only partially completed or totally neglected. Evaluation is very difficult to accomplish, especially for entire curricula or programs; and it usually is very time consuming as well. And finally, practical evaluative techniques for entire curricula and programs do not seem to be very well developed at this time. Nevertheless, an attempt should be made to evaluate any new curriculum or program that is implemented, and that evaluation should be done on a pilot basis first. Therefore, the first evaluation should be for the pilot or on a small scale. Whether a new program is being piloted or implemented into the entire school system, it should be evaluated and the following steps will assist in doing that evaluation.

A. **SPECIFY WHAT IS TO BE EVALUATED—ENTIRE CURRICULUM, SPECIFIC PROGRAM, OR A SPECIFIC SUBJECT AREA, AND FOR WHAT PURPOSE—CONTENT COORDINATION, CONTENT ACHIEVEMENT, ETC.**

The first step in any evaluation process is to state exactly what is to be evaluated. That is, is it the whole curriculum, one of the programs, or one of the subject areas within the curriculum? Exactly what is to be evaluated should be specified so that everyone knows. Then what it is within the area that is to be evaluated should be defined. The intent may be to coordinate the curriculum horizontally and vertically; that is, to determine exactly what is going on at each grade level as well as within each grade. This can be considered a form of curriculum evaluation and to do it, refer to Step I, (Substep B), of this Handbook.

If the purpose of the evaluation is to determine how well something is being done in the curriculum, then the first step is to identify what that something is. That is, what are the purposes, goals, or objectives of that part of the curriculum? Then what actually is being done in the curriculum should be determined and the two compared. Before something can be evaluated, it must first be established what is wanted or intended. So whether or not that which is wanted is stated as goals and objectives, it must be stated in some form. It is impossible to evaluate something until it is known what that something is. Therefore, the writers maintain that the first step to curriculum evaluation is to establish the goals and/or objectives of the curriculum which is to be evaluated, and that the objectives be written in measurable terms. If it is necessary to first develop goals or objectives, the evaluator should see Step II of this Handbook.

B. **DETERMINE CRITERIA TO BE USED TO MAKE THE EVALUATION**

Once that part of the curriculum to be evaluated is identified, criteria by which to make judgments should be established. The evaluator should decide what will be used to determine the worth of that which is being measured. A standard or rule of some type can be used; however, *curriculum planners should be careful when setting standards, especially minimum standards*. They must consider what action will be taken when the standard is not achieved. The writers recommend that, if at all possible, the professionals involved (usually teachers and administrators) decide what criteria are to be used to make judgments about that which is being evaluated.

C. IDENTIFY INFORMATION (DATA) NEEDED FOR THE EVALUATION

Evaluators should make a list of the questions being posed by this evaluation, then attempt to define the information required to answer these questions. Goals and objectives of the area being evaluated will help to identify this information. Goals and objectives indicate what is wanted or intended as well as provide a basis from which to compare and evaluate.

Some of the information needed may already be accumulated and on file. For example, school records and student files may contain pertinent information. Also, education, professional, and testing associations may have data on file that can be used as comparisons or a point of reference. Individuals conducting the evaluation should make certain any information available is located before the process is set in motion to collect it again. Tenbrink (1974) states, "When 'some' information is available, and it is the kind of information you need, and it is likely to be fairly accurate, use it!" (p.14)

D. DECIDE HOW TO COLLECT NEEDED INFORMATION (DATA) FOR THE EVALUATION

Now that the information to be collected is identified, evaluators should decide when and how to go about it. They should specify where the information will be acquired, who will be involved, and how it will be obtained, whether by survey, interview, tests, etc. It is usually good to set a timetable for collecting data. Without one, the entire process can become bogged down and maybe even not completed.

One of the major tasks of collecting information for evaluation purposes is locating a device or instrument for doing it, and it may even be necessary to develop one. To do this, evaluators should go back to the list of information that is needed and simply try to write it in question form (probably questionnaire or test). It is quite possible that tests given by teachers will be sufficient to collect the data. However, if the development of questionnaires or tests is necessary, evaluators should seek help from measurement specialists such as college and university personnel.

The test is one type of instrument that is used widely in collecting evaluative data. The two basic types of tests used are the standardized and criterion-referenced tests. The standardized test is normed to some group, usually nationally, and will give a national comparison. Information about these tests and how to acquire them can be found in measurement departments of most colleges and universities. Also, most school administrators have access to this information. Criterion-referenced tests examine how well specific goals and objectives have been achieved. They can be teacher-made, or to some extent, purchased commercially. Criterion-referenced tests have not been used very extensively by schools, and the techniques for constructing them does not seem to be very well developed at this time. However, teachers construct tests all the time. If they make certain that the tests refer to the specific goals and objectives being used and to some extent what level of achievement will be accepted as attainment of the objectives, they have developed a criterion-referenced test. Teacher-made criterion-referenced tests are probably as good as commercial tests, *especially for evaluation of local programs*. Following are some sources for locating tests of all kinds.

1. College and university measurement departments, guidance departments, and libraries.

2. Three books that can be found in university libraries which list almost all tests in print are:
   - *The Eighth Mental Measurements Yearbooks*, Volumes 1 and 2, by Buros (1978).
   - *Tests in Print II* by Buros (1974).

3. Major educational publishing companies. (School administrators have access to the catalogs and personnel representing these companies.)

4. State and national Departments of Education.

5. Educational and professional associations. (State and national offices.)

One other test that could be used in many states is the competency-based test given at the state level. This test seems to be an attempt to use a combination of the criterion-referenced and standardized tests at the state level. In states where these tests are given, it is possible that the results could be used to help with the evaluation process. However, this would be true only if the tests were designed from the same objectives as the program being evaluated.

By using national standardized tests, state competency-based tests, and locally developed criterion-referenced tests, the program being evaluated can be compared on national, state, and local levels. It can be determined if the program is meeting national, state, and local norms. Special care should be taken when using any type of standardized tests, because they probably have been developed using objectives different from those being used in a specific program. If this is the case, a true measure of what the learner has achieved is not likely.

E. COLLECT AND ANALYZE INFORMATION (DATA) FOR THE EVALUATION

At this point, individuals should proceed with the survey, interviews, administering tests, or what is being done to collect the needed information. Again, evaluators probably should have a set timetable for doing this in order to assure that it is completed. As the data is collected, it should be organized according to some system so that it can be easily analyzed. Cost information should be included in this data if appropriate and possible.

Next, the data should be analyzed and treated statistically if necessary. If the decision makers are different from those who have been collecting the information, data showing the results should be given to them. Those who analyzed the data should be ready to interpret it further if asked to do so by the decision-makers.

F. EVALUATE INFORMATION (DATA) AND MAKE DECISIONS

This is the point at which the actual evaluation takes place. Up to now, testing and other forms of measurement have been done. The difference between measurement and evaluation is that measurement simply states what is happening; with evaluation, judgment is made as to the worth of something, whether it is good, bad, right, wrong, etc. So whoever is charged with the responsibility of making the decision about what is to be done with the results of the measurement, now makes the judgment (evaluation) and the decision about what to do next.

New curricula or programs should be implemented on a pilot basis first. Once piloted, outcomes of the new program should be compared with what was wanted, namely, school and program goals/objectives which would have been developed to meet the curricular need stated in Step I of this planning process. Based on these comparisons, the decision-makers can judge (evaluate) how effective the new program is in meeting this need. Then, depending on how well the new program is meeting the stated curricular need, a decision can be made as to which of the following is to be done:

1. Terminate the new program. (Could consider another new program and pilot it again.)

or

2. Revise the new program and pilot it again. (Often the new program is revised at this point and then, instead of piloting again, it is adopted as part of the permanent curriculum.)

or

3. Adopt new program as part of the permanent curriculum.

If the new program or curriculum is adopted as a permanent part of the school system, those who are going to implement it should go back through the ten steps of this curriculum planning process and determine if any of the Steps need to be done on a larger scale. Since the new program is now probably being planned for the entire school system, more steps may be used and more in depth than for the curriculum study. Steps VIII, Curriculum Design, and IX, Curriculum Implementation, will especially need to be rechecked to determine if these need to be done on an expanded basis.

Note: The public should be kept informed about this curriculum development from the beginning. Now they should be given more specific information about the new program and be made aware that it is becoming a part of the permanent curriculum of the school system.

REFERENCES

Bee, Clifford P. "Guidelines for Designing a School Evaluation." *Educational Technology*, May, 1973, *13*, 44-47.

Buros, Oscar Krisen (Ed.). *Tests in Print II*. Highland Park, NJ: Gryphon Press, 1974.

Buros, Oscar Krisen (Ed.). *The Eighth Mental Measurements Yearbook* (Vol. 1). Highland Park, NJ: Gryphon Press, 1978.

Buros, Oscar Krisen (Ed.). *The Eighth Mental Measurements Yearbook* (Vol. 2). Highland Park, NJ: Gryphon Press, 1978.

Deprospo, Ernest R. and Liesener, James W. "Media Program Evaluation: A Working Framework." *School Media Quarterly*, Summer, 1975, *3*, 289-301.

Doll, Ronald C. *Curriculum Improvement* (4th ed.). Boston: Allyn and Bacon, 1978.

Gephart, William J. "Who Will Engage in Curriculum Evaluation?" *Educational Leadership*, January, 1978, *35*, 284-286.

Hunkins, Francis P. *Curriculum Development: Program Improvement*. Columbus: Charles E. Merrill, 1980.

Hunt, Barbara. "Who and What Are To Be Evaluated?" *Educational Leadership*, January, 1978, *35*, 260-263.

Jacobs, James. "A Model for Program Development and Evaluation." *Theory Into Practice*, February, 1974, *13*, 15-21.

Johnson, James A., and others. *Introduction to the Foundations of American Education* (4th ed.). Boston: Allyn and Bacon, 1979.

Lutterodt, S. A. "A Systematic Approach to Curriculum Evaluation." *Journal of Curriculum Studies*, November, 1975, *7*, 135-150.

Matczynski, Thomas and Rogus, Joseph. "Criteria for Program Analysis." *NASSP Bulletin*, April, 1975, *59*, 44-51.

Neagley, Ross L. and Evans, N. Dean. *Handbook for Effective Curriculum Development*. Englewood Cliffs, NJ: Prentice-Hall, 1967.

Oliver, Albert I. *Curriculum Improvement: A Guide to Problems, Principles, and Process* (2nd ed.). New York: Harper and Row, 1977.

Payne, David A. (Ed.). *Curriculum Evaluation*. Lexington, MA: D. C. Heath, 1974.

Popham, W. James. "An Approaching Peril: Cloud-Referenced Tests." *Phi Delta Kappan*, May, 1974, *55*, 614-615.

Pratt, David. *Curriculum, Design and Development*. New York: Harcourt Brace Jovanovich, 1980.

Ragan, William B. and Shepherd, Gene D. *Modern Elementary Curriculum* (5th ed.). New York: Holt, Rinehart and Winston, 1977.

Rhodes, Gregory L. and Young, Donald B. "Making Curriculum Development Work Again." *Educational Leadership*, May, 1981, *38*, 627-629.

Saylor, Galen J.; Alexander, William M.; and Lewis, Arthur J. *Curriculum Planning for Better Teaching and Learning* (4th ed.). Chicago: Holt, Rinehart and Winston, 1981.

Stufflebeam, Daniel, and others. *Educational Evaluation and Decision Making*. Itasca, IL: F. E. Peacock, 1971.

Tankard, George C., Jr. *Curriculum Improvement: An Administrator's Guide*. West Nyack, NY: Parker, 1974.

Taylor, Peter A. and Cowley, Doris M. *Readings in Curriculum Evaluation*. Dubuque, IA: Wm. C. Brown, 1972.

Tenbrink, Terry D. *Evaluation, A Practical Guide for Teachers*. New York: McGraw-Hill, 1974.

Tennyson, Carol L. and Tennyson, Robert D. "Evaluation in Curriculum Development." *Educational Technology*, September, 1978, *18*, 52-55.

Trump, J. Lloyd and Georgiades, William. "How to Evaluate the Quality of Educational Programs." *NASSP Bulletin*, May, 1975, *59*, 99-103.

Tyler, Louise L. "Curriculum Evaluation and Persons." *Educational Leadership*, January, 1978, *35*, 275-279.

Tyler, Ralph W. "Specific Approaches to Curriculum Development." In James R. Gress and David E. Purpel (Eds.), *Curriculum, An Introduction to the Field*. Berkeley: McCutchan, 1978.

Wiles, Jon and Bondi, Joseph, Jr. *Curriculum Development*. Columbus: Charles E. Merrill, 1979.

Worthen, Blaine R. "Characteristics of Good Evaluating Studies." *Journal of Research and Development in Education*, Spring, 1977, *10*, 3-20.

Zacharewicz, F. A. and Coger, Rich. "Educational Needs Assessment: A Systematic Approach." *Journal of Allied Health*, Winter, 1977, 54-60.

APPENDIX A

CURRICULUM GUIDES: A DEVELOPMENT GUIDE AND CHECKLIST

INTRODUCTION

An educational curriculum guide is an instructional aid that facilitates the teaching/learning process. It is usually more general and suggestive than it is specific and prescriptive. A curriculum guide can, however, be as specific as a teaching unit or lesson plan if that is its purpose and intent. Ordinarily, a guide includes goals, objectives, concepts, and content as well as a variety of learning experiences, teaching aids and resources, instructional procedures, and evaluation techniques.

This Curriculum Guide Development Checklist provides an outline of the items usually included in a guide, with space to check and note plans and progress for each item. The Checklist enables those who are developing curriculum guides to know exactly what they have done, are doing, and considering doing at all times. Writing the curriculum guide is one of the final steps in the curriculum planning and development process. It is a continuous process, and curriculum guides should be constantly reviewed and revised.

The authors make no claims that the Curriculum Guide Development Checklist is all-inclusive. Since curriculum guides may cover one or more grade levels, one or more subject areas, an entire school system, or even a statewide system of education, it is impossible for one checklist to serve as a model for all of them. However, if every item on the Checklist is checked as the development of the guide proceeds, omission of anything major in the guide can be avoided. Also, if the Checklist is followed closely, curriculum guides will be more organized and consistent which will make them easier to read and use.

How To Use This Checklist

Users of the Curriculum Guide Development Checklist should first read through and familiarize themselves with the entire list. Next, they should go through it again, checking the appropriate space for each item as follows: "Considering It"—thinking about doing it but need to study it more; "Planning It" —decided to do it and planning how to do it; "Doing It"—in the process of carrying out the plan; "Completed"—finished prior to this study or just completed; "Not Needed"—not applicable or not needed for this curriculum guide.

The lines following each item on the Checklist can be used to make comments as to why the item was checked a certain way or how the item relates to this particular situation. Therefore, the Checklist can be used to develop curriculum guides for all subject areas and grade levels. If the space for each item on the Checklist is checked as the curriculum guide is developed, an up-to-date record of its progress is provided. Those writing on the Checklist should use a lead pencil so they can erase and change their responses when desired. Also, all pencil writing can be erased and the Checklist used again to develop another guide. If necessary, checkmarks and comments can be written on separate sheets of paper to develop more curriculum guides.

CURRICULUM GUIDE DEVELOPMENT CHECKLIST

	CONSIDERING IT	PLANNING IT	DOING IT	COMPLETED	NOT NEEDED
1. TITLE PAGE INCLUDES:					
A. Title of guide					
B. Name and address of the school system for which the guide is being developed					
C. Grade level(s)					
D. Subject area(s)					
E. Publication date					
2. ACKNOWLEDGMENTS—NOTE THE INDIVIDUALS WHO PLANNED AND PREPARED THE GUIDE. (THIS INFORMATION MAY BE INCLUDED IN THE PREFACE.)					
3. TABLE OF CONTENTS WITH PAGE NUMBERS—MAKES THE GUIDE EASIER TO USE					

	CONSIDERING IT	PLANNING IT	DOING IT	COMPLETED	NOT NEEDED

4. PREFACE OR FOREWORD INCLUDES:

    A. Background—brief statement about why the guide was written

    B. Purpose—what the guide is designed to accomplish

    C. Audience—for whom the guide was written

    D. Signature of the highest administrative official in the school system

5. INTRODUCTION—SPECIFIES HOW TO USE THE GUIDE

6. ORGANIZATION:

    A. Provide a structured and consistent format

    B. Provide space for teacher comments

    C. Provide for adding and replacing pages to encourage revisions

	CONSIDERING IT	PLANNING IT	DOING IT	COMPLETED	NOT NEEDED
7. PHILOSOPHY—STATEMENT OF PHILOSOPHY PERTAINING TO THE TOPIC OF THE GUIDE					
8. GOALS—BROAD, GENERAL STATEMENTS OF INTENDED OUTCOMES OF THE TOPIC OF THE GUIDE					
9. CONTENT:					
A. Include an outline of the basic content of each unit or chapter. (The outline indicates the proposed sequence of instruction as well as the areas of instruction.)					
B. Allow for differing levels of ability and/or cultural backgrounds					
C. Allow for different races and sexes (content does not stereotype the races or sexes)					
D. Suggest supplementary content					
10. OBJECTIVES:					
A. State the unit, chapter, or lesson objectives					

	CONSIDERING IT	PLANNING IT	DOING IT	COMPLETED	NOT NEEDED

B. State objectives in terms of student behavior (may want to state them by domains: cognitive, affective, psychomotor)

11. MATERIALS AND RESOURCES:

A. List required materials and instructional aids

B. Suggest appropriate resource and/or reference materials

C. Suggest appropriate instructional media (films, filmstrips, records)

D. Indicate where instructional media, resource and reference materials are located and how to order or obtain them

12. INSTRUCTIONAL PROCEDURES AND ACTIVITIES:

A. Suggest and describe a variety of teaching methods and instructional techniques appropriate for achieving the stated objectives

B. Suggest and describe a variety of student learning activities and experiences appropriate for achieving the stated objectives

	CONSIDERING IT	PLANNING IT	DOING IT	COMPLETED	NOT NEEDED
C. Suggest procedures and techniques for individualized instruction and independent study					

13. EVALUATION:

A. Describe testing and grading policies					
B. Describe how testing and grading are developed directly from goals and objectives					
C. Suggest procedures (pretests, for example) for appraising student capability and achievement before selecting materials and beginning instruction					
D. Suggest various possible ways of evaluating student progress and achievement of this content					

(Zenger and Zenger, 1973)

REFERENCES

Doll, Ronald C. *Curriculum Improvement* (4th ed.). Boston: Allyn and Bacon, 1978.

Gall, Meredith D. *Handbook for Evaluating and Selecting Curriculum Materials*. Boston: Allyn and Bacon, 1981.

Littrell, J. Harvey and Bailey, Gerald D. "Administrators, Teachers: Stop Writing Curriculum Guides That Won't Be Used!" *NASSP Bulletin*, March, 1981, 29-32.

Saylor, J. Galen; Alexander, William M.; Lewis, Arthur J. *Curriculum Planning for Better Teaching and Learning* (4th ed.). Chicago: Holt, Rinehart and Winston, 1981.

Zenger, Weldon F. and Zenger, Sharon K. *Writing and Evaluating Curriculum Guides*. Belmont, CA: Lear Siegler, Inc./Fearon, 1973.

APPENDIX B

TEXTBOOK EVALUATION: A GUIDE AND CHECKLIST

The first step in the selection of a textbook is to specify in general terms the content wanted. This can be done by listing the goals or general objectives of the course. Another, and probably an easier way, is to list the major concepts, topics, and skills to be covered in the course. Once the major goals or topics to be covered in the course have been identified, they should be cross-checked with the major topics included in each of the textbooks being considered. A form such as the one on the next two pages can be used to make the cross-reference. Also, the form shows a comparison of all the textbooks being evaluated. When the form has been completed for each textbook, the totals should be recorded on the Profile Chart at the end of this evaluation guide on page 123.

READABILITY

Readability as used here refers to the approximate reading grade level of written material. There are numerous standard reading formulas for estimating the reading level of written material. Developers of these formulas acknowledge that they are not exact or absolutely accurate. However, these writers have found the Fry Readability Formula, the one used in this Handbook, to be extremely helpful in the selection of textbooks. It helps to predict how well most students at a given grade level will be able to read each book being considered. To be able to do that before a textbook is adopted makes the Readability Formula of tremendous importance; especially since readability is probably the single most important factor in selecting a classroom textbook. Therefore, readability, along with the major topics covered in the course, is treated first in this process of evaluating textbooks.

TEXTBOOK MAIN TOPICS COMPARISON FORM

TITLES OF TEXTBOOKS BEING EVALUATED

COURSE TITLE:_____

_____

MAJOR CONCEPTS, TOPICS, SKILLS OF THE COURSE	A.	B.	C.	D.	E.	F.	G.	H.	I.	J.
1.										
2.										
3.										
4.										
5.										
6.										
7.										
8.										
9.										
0.										

TEXTBOOK MAIN TOPICS COMPARISON FORM (EXAMPLE)

TITLES OF TEXTBOOKS BEING EVALUATED

COURSE TITLE: Curriculum Planning and Development

MAJOR CONCEPTS, TOPICS SKILLS OF THE COURSE	A. CURRICULUM TOMORROW	B. CURRICULUM PLANNING: A TEN STEP PROCESS	C. SCHOOL PROGRAMS FOR THE FUTURE	D. CURRICULUM BUILDING	E.	F.	G.	H.	I.	J.
1. Curriculum Needs Assessment	X	X		X						
2. Developing Goals and Objectives		X	X	X						
3. Resources and Constraints of Curriculum Development		X								
4. Curriculum Committees for Curriculum Studies	X	X		X						
5. Roles of Personnel in Curriculum Development		X	X							
6. Identifying New Curricula	X	X	X							
7. Selecting New Curricula		X	X	X						
8. Curriculum Design	X	X		X						
9. Curriculum Implementation		X								
10. Curriculum Evaluation		X								

Since readability is one of the most (if not the most) important factors in the selection of a textbook, it is placed before the Textbook Evaluation Checklist. It may be advisable, however, to evaluate a prospective textbook using the Checklist before doing a readability estimate. If the textbook is eliminated for other reasons, time will not have been spent determining its readability. Once the reading grade level has been calculated, record it on the Profile Chart at the end of the Checklist.

FRY READABILITY FORMULA

The Fry Readability Formula can be used to determine the approximate reading grade level of textbooks as well as other written materials. By checking the approximate reading grade level of material with the Fry Formula, educators can better determine if the material (textbook) is appropriate for their students. The Fry Procedure is a device for measuring the difficulty of printed material based on word and sentence length.

CAUTION: This procedure is an estimate and should not be taken as an exact absolute for determining the reading grade level of written material. It does give a close indication of the reading level and certainly should be a part of evaluating and selecting textbooks.

I. FRY READABILITY PROCEDURE

The Fry Readability Graph shows the approximate reading grade level of printed material by measuring two factors, word length and sentence length.

Expanded Directions for Using Fry's Graph for Estimating Readability-Extended
(These directions are illustrated step-by-step in the following pages.)

1. Randomly select (3) three sample passages and count out exactly 100 words beginning with the beginning of a sentence. Do count proper nouns, initializations, and numerals.

2. Count the number of sentences in the hundred words, estimating length of the fraction of the last sentence to the nearest 1/10th.

3. Count the total number of syllables in the 100-word passage. If you don't have a hand counter available, an easy way is to simply put a mark above every syllable over one in each word, then when you get to the end of the passage, count the number of marks and add 100. Small calculators can also be used as counters by pushing numeral "1", then push the "+" sign for each word or syllable when counting.

4. Enter graph with *average* sentence length and *average* number of syllables; plot dot where the two lines intersect. Area where dot is plotted will give you the approximate grade level.

5. If a great deal of variability is found in syllable count or sentence count, putting more samples into the average is desirable.

6.   A word is defined as a group of symbols with a space on either side; thus, "Joe," "IRA," "1945," and "&" are each one word.

7.   A syllable is defined as a phonetic syllable. Generally, there are as many syllables as vowel sounds. For example, "stopped" is one syllable and "wanted" is two syllables. When counting syllables for numerals and initializations, count one syllable for each symbol. For example, "1945" is 4 syllables, and "IRA" is 3 syllables, and "&" is 1 syllable.

How to Count Sentences in a Sample

Count as a sentence each unit of thought marked by end punctuation. This can be done by following the punctuation marks. Count as a sentence if it is separated by a period, question mark, or exclamation point. Examples:

What was the topic discussed? Pollution. (two sentences)

Water is an absolute necessity for survival; entertainment is not. (one sentence)

There are two reasons for not buying the coat: (1) You don't need it. (2) It costs too much. (one sentence)

He ran, but he still could not escape. (one sentence)

The students in the English class worked diligently, and they all finished their work early. (one sentence)

Four people were at the party: Shirley, Mary, Bob, and Jack. (one sentence)

A Sample Sentence Count

(Start)   Each teacher must decide which method he will use for particular situations. (1) Several factors which should be considered include his teaching objectives, his abilities, limitations, skills, and knowledge of the subject, the students' intelligence levels, abilities, interests and backgrounds, the number of students, the availability of materials and equipment, school facilities, and school policy. (2)

This book is designed to give teachers a quick cookbook approach to a variety of methods from which they can choose. (3) Each method or way of teaching has a brief definition and main purpose, how it works or how to use procedures, guidelines for using, examples, (Stop) advantages, and disadvantages. (4) (Zenger and Zenger, 1977, pp. 1-2)

25 words in final sentence fragment	divided by	28 total number of words in final sentence	equal	.9 final sentence fragment estimated to nearest tenth of a full sentence

Number of sentences: 3.9

How to Count Syllables in a Sample

Each vowel sound represents one syllable. Examples:

ball (1)	can/cer (2)	a/ble (2)
a/re/a (3)	ac/com/mo/date (4)	can/dy (2)

Prefixes and suffixes such as pre-, un-, -ment, -ed, and -ly usually form a syllable. Examples:

Prefixes

pre/school (2)

un/a/ble (3)

Suffixes

pay/ment (2)

land/ed (2)

slow/ly (2)

Sample syllable counts follow on page 101.

A Sample Syllable Count

(Start) Each teacher must decide which method he will use for particular   17
situations. Several factors which should be considered include his teaching   20
objectives, his abilities, limitations, skills, and knowledge of the subject,   20
the students' intelligence levels, abilities, interests and backgrounds, the   20
number of students, the availability of materials and equipment, school   22
facilities, and school policy.   9

This book is designed to give teachers a quick cookbook approach to a   17
variety of methods from which they can choose. Each method or way of teaching   20
has a brief definition and main purpose, how it works or how to use procedures,   21
guidelines for using, examples, (Stop) advantages, and disadvantages.   8

(Zenger and Zenger, 1977, pp. 1-2)   174

Number of syllables 174

A Sample Syllable Count by the Quick Method

Just count every syllable over one per word and then add 100:

(Start) Each teacher must decide which method he will use for particular   6
situations. Several factors which should be considered include his teaching   10
objectives, his abilities, limitations, skills, and knowledge of the subject,   10
the students' intelligence levels, abilities, interests and backgrounds, the   11
number of students, the availability of materials and equipment, school   12
facilities, and school policy.   5

This book is designed to give teachers a quick cookbook approach to a   4
variety of methods from which they can choose. Each method or way of teaching   6
has a brief definition and main purpose, how it works or how to use procedures,   6
guidelines for using, examples, (Stop) advantages, and disadvantages.   4

(Zenger and Zenger, 1977, pp. 1-2)   74

74 syllables over one per word + 100 = 174

Number of syllables 174

101

How to Graph and Chart the Results

Assume that the above process has been repeated for two more samples and the total results are as follows:

Sample	No. of Sentences per 100 words	No. of Syllables per 100 words
I	3.9	174
II	3.9	174
III	3.8	144
	11.6	492

Find the averages: $11.6 \div 3 = 3.9$ $492 \div 3 = 164$

To find the approximate reading grade level, refer to the Readability Graph on page 103.

1. Locate the average sentence length at the left edge of the graph. For our example, it is 3.9 .

2. Locate the average number of syllables at the top edge of the graph. For our example, it is 164 .

3. Follow the pertinent row and column on the graph until the two intersect. Plot a dot at the intersection. The area where the dot is located indicates the approximate grade level of the sampled reading matter. For our example, the approximate reading grade level is 13 .

4. If a large amount of variability is found, enter more sample counts into the average.

CAUTION:
According to Dr. Fry, this is an estimate within one grade level in either direction. For example, a textbook may use very technical or difficult vocabulary but extremely short sentences. In such a case, the results of the Fry Readability Graph may underestimate the actual difficulty level of the text.

GRAPH FOR ESTIMATING READABILITY — EXTENDED
by Edward Fry, Rutgers University Reading Center, New Brunswick, N.J. 08904

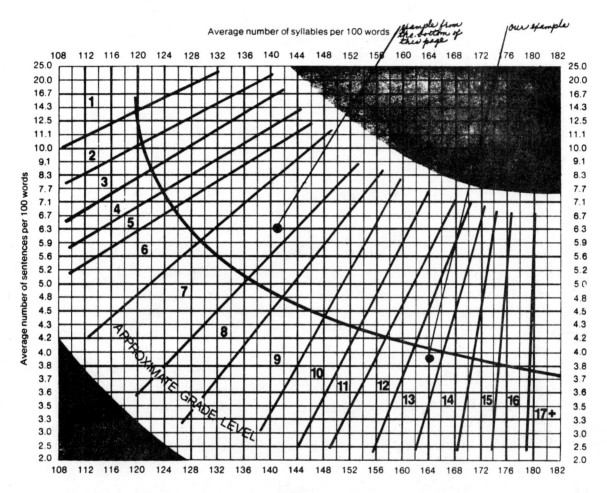

DIRECTIONS: Randomly select 3 one hundred word passages from a book or an article. Plot average number of syllables and average number of sentences per 100 words on graph to determine the grade level of the material. Choose more passages per book if great variability is observed and conclude that the book has uneven readability. Few books will fall in gray area but when they do grade level scores are invalid.

Count proper nouns, numerals and initializations as words. Count a syllable for each symbol. For example, "1945" is 1 word and 4 syllables and "IRA" is 1 word and 3 syllables.

EXAMPLE:		SYLLABLES	SENTENCES
	1st Hundred Words	124	6.6
	2nd Hundred Words	141	5.5
	3rd Hundred Words	158	6.8
	AVERAGE	141	6.3

READABILITY 7th GRADE (see dot plotted on graph)

For further information and validity data see the Journal of Reading December, 1977.

HOW TO USE THIS TEXTBOOK EVALUATION CHECKLIST

For each item listed in the Checklist, there is a place to check the rating from **Excellent** to **Poor** as well as a space to mark **Not Included** and **Not Applicable**.

Not Included means that the item should have been included in the textbook but was not, and the evaluator should check the appropriate space in the column labeled **Not Included**.

Not Applicable means that the given material does not apply to the textbook being evaluated, or that it has already been evaluated in another part of the Checklist.

Each individual who evaluates the items listed in this Checklist will have a different interpretation of what is meant by **Excellent** or **Poor**. This difference in interpretation does not limit the evaluations, however, because the primary purpose of these guidelines is to assist educators in judging how useful the textbook would be to them in their own particular situation. For example, when a teacher checks an item **Excellent**, he/she is saying that that particular part of the textbook will be very useful for his/her teaching.

Since the items listed are general in nature and are considered common to all types of textbooks, space has been provided at the end of each section for additional items to be filled in by the evaluator. These items will probably relate to specific subject areas. Also there is space for comments after each item, as well as additional space for general comments at the end of each section. The fact that space has been provided does not mean, however, that comments have to be made after each item. The space is provided in case the evaluator wants to add a note in addition to checking one of the rating classifications. The space provided for comments at the end of each section is for any comments or questions the evaluator might have concerning that particular group of items.

The authors recommend that the rating scale be checked in pencil so that the responses can be changed. As the evaluator goes over the items a second time or compares them with those of other evaluators, he/she may wish to change his/her ratings. The rating scale may be used for evaluating more than one book by identifying each textbook with a different capital letter. At least two books can be evaluated on each rating scale. Also, if a pencil is used, the response can be erased and the rating scale used again.

Example of checking the rating scale for two books is on the next page:

I.

AUTHORSHIP

(Checkmarks A and B indicate separate textbooks. Their titles will be on the first page of the Checklist.)

	EXCELLENT	GOOD	ACCEPTABLE	POOR	NOT INCLUDED	NOT APPLICABLE
A. Author's purpose in writing the textbook: 　1. Stated clearly (probably in the preface or introduction of Teacher's Edition)	B		A			
2. Suitable for subject area	A B					
B. Author has background qualifications and/or experience in the subject area (may have to write the publisher for this)		B	A			

To total the findings, use the Profile Charts at the end of this evaluation form. Count the number checked in each rating classification for each category and enter it in the proper column on the profile Chart. Total the number in each column and enter it at the bottom of the chart where indicated.

Example on next page:

TEXTBOOK EVALUATION PROFILE CHART

Title of Textbook		EXCELLENT	GOOD	ACCEPTABLE	POOR	NOT INCLUDED	NOT APPLICABLE
I. Authorship	Book A	1	1	1			
	Book B	2	1				
II. General Characteristics		5	2	2	1		
		8	2				
III. Physical and Mechanical Features		10	3	1	3		
		14	2	1			
IV. Philosophy		4	1	2		2	
		7	1	1			
V. Organization of Material		1	1	1			
		3					
VI. Objectives		1		1		2	
		3	1				
VII. Subject-Matter Content		8	1		2		
		10	1				
VIII. Teaching Aids and Supplementary Material		1	2	2		3	4
		5	2			1	4
IX. Teacher's Edition or Manual		2	1	1		3	
		5	1			1	
TOTAL NUMBER IN EACH RATING CLASSIFICATION FOR ALL CATEGORIES	Book A	33	12	12	6	10	4
	Book B	57	10	2	0	2	4

Calculated reading grade level . . . . Book A 14 College level
Book B 17^{+} graduate level

Number of course topics covered by this textbook . Book A 4
Book B 10

Comments:

106

Now, by noting the totals for each rating classification, an evaluation of the entire textbook can be made. Also, each category may be evaluated separately by noting the number entered in each rating classification between the horizontal lines. Textbooks may be compared with each other by using the Profile Chart for each textbook and placing them side by side so the nine categories are in line. This way the textbook can be compared category by category or by the total of all categories. The two separate categories, readability and number of course topics included in the textbook, can also be compared.

An example of how to further summarize and explain the Profile Chart follows the Profile Chart at the end of this Checklist on page 124.

TEXTBOOK EVALUATION CHECKLIST

(Textbook A)

TITLE OF TEXTBOOK___(Textbook B)_____

_____

AUTHOR(S)_____

GRADE LEVEL(S)_____

SUBJECT AREA_____

PUBLISHER_____

COPYRIGHT DATE_____

EVALUATOR_____

DATE REVIEWED_____

COMMENTS:

I.

AUTHORSHIP

	EXCELLENT	GOOD	ACCEPTABLE	POOR	NOT INCLUDED	NOT APPLICABLE
A. Author's purpose in writing the textbook: 1. Stated clearly (probably in the preface or introduction of Teacher's Edition)						
2. Suitable for the subject area						
B. Author has background qualifications and/or experience in the subject area (may have to write the publisher for this)						
Additional items to be filled in by evaluator, especially for specific subjects:						
C. _____						
D. _____						
Comments:						

II.

GENERAL CHARACTERISTICS

		EXCELLENT	GOOD	ACCEPTABLE	POOR	NOT INCLUDED	NOT APPLICABLE
A.	Current publication data (check carefully if more than five years old)						
	1. Material is actually as recent as publication date indicates						
	2. If text is revised publication, new version reflects significant changes rather than a few changed words						
B.	Attractive appearance enriched with up-to-date illustrations						
C.	Written in clear, concise form						
	1. Includes explanations of technical terms and details						
	2. Uses examples to explain material						
	3. Uses correct grammar						
D.	Cost: Available from publisher 1. Reasonable initial cost						
	2. Reasonable ongoing costs—for workbooks, lab sheets, etc., used with material on hand						

II.

GENERAL CHARACTERISTICS (Continued)

	EXCELLENT	GOOD	ACCEPTABLE	POOR	NOT INCLUDED	NOT APPLICABLE

Additional items to be filled in by evaluator, especially for specific subjects:

E. _____

_____

F. _____

_____

Comments:

III.

PHYSICAL AND MECHANICAL FEATURES

A. Page:
    1. Appropriate Size:

B. Cover:
    1. Durable

III.

PHYSICAL AND MECHANICAL FEATURES (Continued)

	EXCELLENT	GOOD	ACCEPTABLE	POOR	NOT INCLUDED	NOT APPLICABLE
B. Cover (Continued) 2. Attractive						
C. Binding: 1. Appears durable, able to withstand several years' use						
2. Allows cover and pages to open flat after broken in (this usually means a better binding)						
D. Paper: 1. Quality						
2. If tinted, has appropriate tint						
E. Type: 1. Size appropriate for grade level to avoid eyestrain						
2. Attractive						
3. Variation in type appropriate for clear presentation and attractive appearance						
F. Spacing: 1. Words properly spaced and lined for easy reading						

III.

PHYSICAL AND MECHANICAL FEATURES (Continued)

	EXCELLENT	GOOD	ACCEPTABLE	POOR	NOT INCLUDED	NOT APPLICABLE
F. Spacing (Continued) 2. Margins on outer and inner edges of page wide enough						
G. Illustrations: 1. Appropriate for interest and grade level						
2. Presents true picture of today's society						
3. Placed near reference in text						
H. Tables, graphs, and charts: 1. Placed near reference in text						
2. Appropriate for interest and grade level						
Additional items to be filled in by evaluator, especially for specific subjects:						
I. _____						
J. _____						
Comments:						

IV.

PHILOSOPHY OF THE MATERIAL PRESENTED

This section may be examined in the present sequence, but preferably finished after completing the subject-matter content section.

	EXCELLENT	GOOD	ACCEPTABLE	POOR	NOT INCLUDED	NOT APPLICABLE
A. Philosophy: 1. Clearly stated (probably in the preface or introduction of Teacher's Edition)						
2. Acceptable to the community. (If philosophy is not stated, base judgment on what you think it is.)						
B. Avoids biases and prejudices						
C. Material dealing with the following acceptable to the school and community: 1. Race						
2. Religion						
3. Sex						
D. Promotes a positive self-image for all social groups and individuals (avoids stereotyping the sexes and races)						
E. Treats controversial issues factually and in a scholarly manner						
F. Does not use swearing, profanity, and vulgarity						

IV.

PHILOSOPHY (Continued)

Additional items to be filled in by evaluator, especially for specific subjects:

	EXCELLENT	GOOD	ACCEPTABLE	POOR	NOT INCLUDED	NOT APPLICABLE
G. _____						
_____						
H. _____						
Comments						

V.

ORGANIZATION OF MATERIAL

	EXCELLENT	GOOD	ACCEPTABLE	POOR	NOT INCLUDED	NOT APPLICABLE
A. Organizes material clearly						
B. Organizes material in logical sequence						
C. Provides continuity between lessons, chapters, and units						

V.

ORGANIZATION OF MATERIAL (Continued)

	EXCELLENT	GOOD	ACCEPTABLE	POOR	NOT INCLUDED	NOT APPLICABLE
Additional items to be filled in by evaluator, especially for specific subjects:						
D. _____						
_____						
E. _____						
Comments:						

VI.

OBJECTIVES

	EXCELLENT	GOOD	ACCEPTABLE	POOR	NOT INCLUDED	NOT APPLICABLE
A. Specific student objectives of each lesson, chapter, or unit (probably in Teacher's Edition):						
1. Clearly stated						
2. Contributes to and develops most objectives of the course (if not stated, judge based on your concept of the objectives of the material						

VI.

OBJECTIVES (Continued)

	EXCELLENT	GOOD	ACCEPTABLE	POOR	NOT INCLUDED	NOT APPLICABLE
B. Accompanying problems, exercises, tests, and other aids, directly or indirectly develop the objectives						
Additional items to be filled in by evaluator, especially for specific subjects:						
C. _____						
D. _____						
Comments:						

VII.

SUBJECT-MATTER CONTENT

	EXCELLENT	GOOD	ACCEPTABLE	POOR	NOT INCLUDED	NOT APPLICABLE
A. Fulfills most objectives of the course						
B. Presents material correctly and truthfully						

VII.

SUBJECT-MATTER CONTENT (Continued)

	EXCELLENT	GOOD	ACCEPTABLE	POOR	NOT INCLUDED	NOT APPLICABLE
C. Has been field tested or learner verified						
D. Avoids stereotyping of the: 1. Sexes—Language and pictures						
2. Races—Language and pictures						
E. Provides sufficient coverage of content						
F. Provides sufficient coverage of skills						
G. Uses proper terminology						
H. Defines terms accurately						
I. Interest level suitable for grade level						
J. Provides for individual differences						
Additional items to be filled in by evaluator, especially for specific subjects:						
K. _____						

VII.

SUBJECT-MATTER CONTENT (Continued)

Additional items (Continued)

	EXCELLENT	GOOD	ACCEPTABLE	POOR	NOT INCLUDED	NOT APPLICABLE
L. _____						
_____						
Comments:						

VIII.

TEACHING AIDS AND SUPPLEMENTARY MATERIAL

A. For each lesson, chapter, unit, or other subdivision, includes appropriate:
1. Activities

2. Exercises and/or drills

3. Questions

4. Problems

VIII.

TEACHING AIDS AND SUPPLEMENTARY MATERIAL (Continued)

	EXCELLENT	GOOD	ACCEPTABLE	POOR	NOT INCLUDED	NOT APPLICABLE
A. (Continued) 5. Individualized teaching instructions						
B. Includes necessary aids to accompany the basic materials						
C. Includes supplementary list of: 1. Readings						
2. Audiovisual aids						
3. Other library resources						
D. Provides appropriate testing materials to accompany the basic material						
F. Provides a suitable and useful workbook						
Additional items to be filled in by evaluator, especially for specific subjects: G. _____						
H. _____						

	EXCELLENT	GOOD	ACCEPTABLE	POOR	NOT INCLUDED	NOT APPLICABLE

VIII.

TEACHING AIDS AND SUPPLEMENTARY MATERIAL (Continued)

Comments:

IX.

TEACHER'S EDITION OR MANUAL

A. Includes a reproduction of each page of the student textbook for teacher's convenience						
B. States the specific objectives for each lesson, chapter, or unit						
C. Provides a list of materials needed for each lesson, chapter, or unit						
D. Suggests practical activities and exercises for each lesson, chapter, or unit						
E. Suggests enrichment and/or remedial activities and exercises for students of varying backgrounds and abilities						

IX.

TEACHER'S EDITION OR MANUAL (Continued)

	EXCELLENT	GOOD	ACCEPTABLE	POOR	NOT INCLUDED	NOT APPLICABLE
F. Provides answers to all problems, questions, or exercises						
G. Provides supplementary information for teachers						
Additional items to be filled in by evaluator, especially for specific subjects:						
H. _____						
I. _____						
Comments:						

TEXTBOOK EVALUATION PROFILE CHART

Title of Textbook

	EXCELLENT	GOOD	ACCEPTABLE	POOR	NOT INCLUDED	NOT APPLICABLE
I. Authorship						
II. General Characteristics						
III. Physical and Mechanical Features						
IV. Philosophy						
V. Organization of Material						
VI. Objectives						
VII. Subject-Matter Content						
VIII. Teaching Aids and Supplementary Material						
IX. Teacher's Edition or Manual						
TOTAL NUMBER OF EACH RATING CLASSIFICATION FOR ALL CATEGORIES						

Calculated reading grade level. . . ._____
Number of course topics covered by this textbook. . . ._____

(Zenger and Zenger, 1976)

TEXTBOOK EVALUATION SUMMARY — ONE EXAMPLE

TOTAL PROFILE CHART RATINGS

TITLE OF TEXTBOOK

	EXCELLENT	GOOD	ACCEPTABLE	POOR	NOT INCLUDED	CALCULATED READING GRADE LEVEL	NUMBER OF COURSE TOPICS COVERED BY THIS TEXTBOOK
A. Curriculum Tomorrow	33	11	11	6	10	14	4

44   17

B. Curriculum Planning: A Ten Step Process	57	10	2	0	2	17+	10

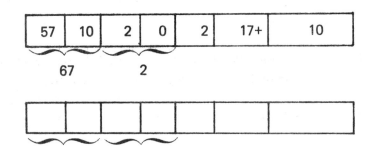

67   2

C.

My first choice for these two textbooks is ___B___. Following are my reasons:

1. The calculated readability is right on grade level, the other one is not.
2. It includes more of the topics covered in the course than the other one.
3. Student objectives are stated for each chapter. Textbook A does not.
4. As can be seen by the Profile Summary Chart, Textbook B is stronger overall than Textbook A. Textbook A has many more items checked acceptable, poor, and not included; while Textbook B has many more items checked excellent and good.

The above are sample summary comments. There can be as many as are necessary to summarize what has been recorded for each textbook evaluated. The summary should include information from the Profile Chart and comments made by the evaluator.

GUIDELINES FOR HANDLING TEXTBOOK COMPLAINTS

Since giving guidelines for handling textbook complaints has not been a major intent of this Handbook, the following is not an exhaustive list of guidelines. However, the suggestions should serve as a starting point for developing procedures for handling textbook complaints.

1. Have a set policy for handling textbook complaints (involve the citizens of the community in establishing this policy).

2. Follow the textbook—complaint policy in handling all complaints (citizens should probably be involved in this stage of action also).

3. Do not remove books from use until they have been banned through the procedures of the complaint policy.

4. Give objectors an out, especially while the complaint is being handled; that is, allow for students to be excused from using the objectionable book or material.

5. Have complaints put in writing and signed. This complaint document should include the title of the specific material that is being questioned and the reasons for complaint. It may be advisable to use a standard complaint form to be completed and signed.

6. Have all school personnel who are in a position to receive textbook complaints prepared to handle them.

7. Have material on file as to how and why any textbook was chosen. (Filing the Profile Charts of this evaluating process would be a quick, easy way of storing such information.)

8. A precautionary measure: Have established guidelines for selecting and adopting instructional material. Also the use of an evaluation process such as the one in this Handbook will help prevent or settle complaints.

(Zenger and Zenger, 1976)

REFERENCES

Barber, Elizabeth and Warming, Eloise. "Touchstones for Textbook Selection." *Phi Delta Kappan*, June, 1980, 694-695.

English, Raymond. "The Politics of Textbook Adoption." *Phi Delta Kappan*, December, 1980, 275-278.

EPIE Institute. *Pilot Guildelines for Improving Instructional Materials Through the Process of Learner Verification and Revision*. New York: EPIE Institute, 1975.

Fry, Edward. "Fry's Readability Graph: Clarifications, Validity, and Extension to Level 17." *Journal of Reading*, December, 1977, 242-252.

Gall, Meredith D. *Handbook for Evaluating and Selecting Curriculum Materials*. Boston: Allyn and Bacon, 1981.

Garcia, Jesus and Armstrong, David G. "Textbook Evaluation: A Simple Procedure for Identifying Treatment of Selected Groups." *The Social Studies*, January-February, 1979, 32-37.

Hallenbeck, Margaret. "How to Serve Successfully on a Textbook Selecting Committee." *The American School Board Journal*, August, 1980, 21-22, 40.

Hefley, James C. *Textbooks on Trial*. Wheaton, IL: Victor Books, 1976.

Kahn, Michael S. "The Selection of a Textbook: Rationale and Evaluation Form." *The Clearing House*, January, 1978, 245-247.

Klein, M. Frances. *About Learning Materials*. Washington, D.C.: Association for Supervision and Curriculum Development, 1978.

Komoski, Kenneth P. "The Realities of Choosing and Using Instructional Materials." *Educational Leadership*, October, 1978, 46-50.

Saylor, J. Galen; Alexander, William M.; Lewis, Arthur J. *Curriculum Planning for Better Teaching and Learning* (4th ed.). Chicago: Holt, Rinehart and Winston, 1981.

Scriptor Pseudonymous. "The Ghost Behind the Classroom Door." *Today's Education*, April-May, 1978, 41-45.

United States Commission on Civil Rights. *Fair Textbooks: A Resource Guide*. Clearinghouse Publication 61. Washington, D.C.: Government Printing Office, 1979.

Woodbury, Mards. *Selecting Instructional Materials*. Bloomington, IN: Phi Delta Kappa, 1978.

Woods, L. B. "Censorship in the Schools." *Phi Delta Kappan*, January, 1980, 10-12.

Zenger, Sharon K. and Zenger, Weldon F. *57 Ways To Teach*. Los Angeles, CA: Crescent, 1977.

Zenger, Weldon F. and Zenger, Sharon K. *Evaluating and Selecting Textbooks*. Belmont, CA: Fearon-Pitman, 1976.

Zenger, Weldon F. and Zenger, Sharon K. *Writing and Evaluating Curriculum Guides*. Belmont, CA: Lear Siegler, Inc./Fearon, 1973.

APPENDIX C

UNIT EXAMPLE

Grade: 10-12   Course/Subject: Contemporary Home Economics

Unit Topic: Pizza with Yeast Dough Crust   Approximate Time Required: One week

1. Main Purpose of the Unit:
       The purpose of this unit is to acquaint the students with the principles of making yeast dough by making pizza. The historical background, nutritional value, and variations of pizza will also be covered.

2. Behavioral Objectives
    The student will be able to:
    1. Explain the functions of each of the ingredients in yeast dough. (Cognitive-comprehension)
    2. Describe the steps in preparing yeast dough. (Cognitive-comprehension)
    3. Make a yeast dough for a pizza crust. (Cognitive-application and psychomotor)
    4. State briefly the history of pizza. (Cognitive-knowledge)
    5. Match the ingredients in pizza to the food groups they represent. (Cognitive-knowledge)
    6. Give examples of different types of pizza. (Cognitive-comprehension)
    7. Create and bake a pizza of their choice. (Cognitive synthesis and psychomotor)

3. Content Outline
    A. Essential ingredients in yeast dough
        (1) Flour
        (2) Yeast
        (3) Liquid
        (4) Sugar
        (5) Salt
    B. Non-essential ingredients
        (1) Fats
        (2) Eggs
        (3) Other, such as fruit and nuts
    C. Preparing yeast dough
        (1) Mixing
        (2) Kneading
        (3) Rising (fermenting)
        (4) Punching down
        (5) Shaping
        (6) Baking
    D. History of pizza
        (1) First pizza was from Naples.
        (2) Pizza is an Italian word meaning pie.
        (3) Originally eaten by the poor, pizza was also enjoyed by royalty.
        (4) Italian immigrants brought pizza to the United States in the late 1800's.
    E. Types of pizza
        (1) Neapolitan

        (2) Sicilian
        (3) Pizza Rustica
        (4) Pizza di Polenta
    F. Nutritional value of pizza
        (1) Nutritious meal or snack
        (2) Can contain all four food groups
        (3) One serving of cheese pizza contains:
            (a) Protein
            (b) Vitamins
            (c) Minerals
    G. Making a pizza
        (1) Prepare dough
        (2) Roll out dough
        (3) Transfer to pan
        (4) Spread sauce
        (5) Top as desired
        (6) Bake

4. Procedures and Activities
    A. Informal lecture
    B. Discussion
    C. Demonstration of mixing and kneading dough
    D. Filmstrip on pizza
    E. Educational game (Pizzeria): Each time a student answers correctly a question about yeast dough or pizza, he gets a part of a paper pizza. The first to collect a complete pizza wins.
    F. Cooking lab

5. Instructional Aids or Resources
    A. Text: *Guide to Modern Meals* (Webster McGraw-Hill, 1970)
    B. Filmstrip: *Pizza, Pizza* 10 minutes
    C. *Pizza, Pizza* booklets by Chef Boyardee
    D. Educational game (Pizzeria)
    E. *Bake-it-easy Yeast Book* by Fleischmann's Yeast
    F. Poster (showing different kinds of pizza) from Pizza Hut

6. Evaluation
    A. Unit test
    B. Lab performance

Unit Test

Yeast Dough and Pizza

Match the pizza ingredient in Column A to the Four Basic Food Groups in Column B. (Cognitive-Knowledge)

Column A	Column B
_____1. Tomato sauce	A. Bread and Cereal Group
_____2. Pepperoni	B. Fruit and Vegetable Group
_____3. Mozzarella Cheese	C. Meat and Protein Group
_____4. Pizza crust	D. Milk and Dairy Group
_____5. Green peppers	

Column A (continued)
_____6. Parmesan Cheese
_____7. Sausage
_____8. Onions

Fill in the blank to the left of each statement with the best word or words to complete the statement. (Cognitive-Knowledge)

_____ 1. Pizza is an Italian word that means __(1)__.

_____ 2. When yeast ferments, it releases __(2)__ gas.

_____ 3. The sudden rising of dough in a heated oven is called __(3)__.

_____ 4. Pizzas were believed to be introduced to America in the late __(4)__.

_____ 5. After yeast dough has risen to double its size, you need to __(5)__ the dough.

Explain the difference between the Rapidmix method and Conventional method of yeast dough preparation. (Cognitive-Comprehension)

Name two types of pizza and describe them. (Cognitive-Comprehension)

Listed below are ingredients found in yeast dough. Explain the function of each of the ingredients. (Cognitive-Comprehension)

1. Flour

2. Yeast

3. Liquid

4. Sugar

5. Salt

Tell in your own words the five key points of kneading yeast dough. (Cognitive-Comprehension)

(Used with permission of Anita Pfannenstiel, student teacher, who followed the conventional unit plan form as presented by Kim and Kellough, 1978.)

REFERENCES

Hunkins, Francis P. *Curriculum Development: Program Improvement*. Columbus: Charles E. Merrill, 1980.

Kim, Eugene C. and Kellough, Richard D. *A Resource Guide for Secondary Teaching* (2nd ed.). Macmillan, 1978.

Pfannenstiel, Anita. "Unit Example." Unpublished course work, Hays, KS, 1982.

Pratt, David. *Curriculum, Design and Development*. New York: Harcourt Brace Jovanovich, 1980.

Saylor, Galen J.; Alexander, William M.; and Lewis, Arthur J. *Curriculum Planning for Better Teaching and Learning* (4th ed.). Chicago: Holt, Rinehart and Winston, 1981.

APPENDIX D

(SIMULATED STUDY)

CENTERVILLE PUBLIC SCHOOL SYSTEM

READING PROGRAM NEEDS ASSESSMENT USING STEP I
OF THE TEN-STEP PROCESS AS A GUIDE

TEACHERS AT THE CENTERVILLE MIDDLE SCHOOL COMPLAIN EVERY YEAR THAT THE INCOMING SIXTH GRADE STUDENTS CANNOT READ AS WELL AS THEY SHOULD. THIS YEAR THEY TOOK THEIR COMPLAINT TO THE DISTRICT CURRICULUM COUNCIL. THE COUNCIL RECOMMENDED THAT A STUDY BE DONE TO DETERMINE IF THERE IS A PROBLEM, AND, IF SO, WHAT IS NEEDED TO CORRECT IT. THEY ALSO RECOMMENDED THAT MR. KING, PRINCIPAL OF WEST ELEMENTARY SCHOOL, BE IN CHARGE OF THE STUDY.

USING STEP I OF THE TEN-STEP CURRICULUM PLANNING PROCESS AS A GUIDE, SET UP A PLAN AS TO HOW THIS NEEDS ASSESSMENT COULD BE ACCOMPLISHED. CHECK THE SPACE ON THE NEEDS ASSESSMENT CHECKLIST PAGE INDICATING WHAT YOU INTEND TO DO FOR EACH SUBSTEP. THEN, ON A SEPARATE SHEET OF PAPER, DESCRIBE HOW YOU WILL CARRY OUT WHAT YOU HAVE CHECKED FOR EACH SUBSTEP. REMEMBER, YOU ARE NOT TO CONDUCT THE NEEDS ASSESSMENT; MERELY PLAN THE STEPS FOR HOW YOU WOULD DO IT.

CENTERVILLE PUBLIC SCHOOL SYSTEM

The Centerville Public School System consists of one high school, one middle school, and three elementary schools. The system has a superintendent, an assistant superintendent in charge of personnel and curriculum, and a principal in each of the five schools. Mrs. Doe, the assistant superintendent, is quite busy wearing two hats. Therefore, she has organized a district curriculum council. A curriculum council is somewhat unusual for a school district this small; however, Mrs. Doe uses it to do much of the curriculum work she would otherwise have to do.

The Centerville School System is considered a good school system by the community. Members of the community seldom ask questions about what the schools are doing and generally support what they do, including financial support. Since what the schools do is never really questioned, teachers, most of the time, are left on their own to decide what to do in their classes. The teachers are generally considered good teachers and usually recceive the teaching material and equipment they request. There is very little staff turnover in Centerville, and the teachers are older and more experienced than in most school systems.

Mrs. Doe has a good working relationship with all the school principals. They respect and usually support each other. Mrs. Doe prefers to operate as a staff officer; however, she does not hesitate to use her line officer authority if necessary. Mrs. Doe also has the respect and support of the school superintendent.

(ONE WAY THE CHECKLIST COULD BE MARKED AND THE NEEDS ASSESSMENT PLANNED WITH THE INFORMATION GIVEN)

STEP I

	CONSIDERING IT	PLANNING IT	DOING IT	COMPLETED	NOT NEEDED
I. STATE THE CURRICULUM PROBLEM OR NEED—CONDUCT A NEEDS ASSESSMENT IF NECESSARY.					
A. IDENTIFY PROBLEM OR NEED					
1. IF KNOWN, STATE THE CURRICULUM PROBLEM OR NEED				✓	
2. IF THE NEED IS UNKNOWN OR SHOULD BE VERIFIED, CONDUCT NEEDS ASSESSMENT	✓				
a. DETERMINE WHAT IS PRESENTLY BEING DONE (WHAT NOW EXISTS), IF ANYTHING	✓				
b. DETERMINE WHAT IS WANTED OR INTENDED	✓				
c. SELECT OR DEVELOP DATA-GATHERING INSTRUMENT (QUESTIONNAIRE, INTERVIEW GUIDE)					✓
d. COLLECT AND ORGANIZE INFORMATION	✓				
e. ANALYZE DATA; COMPARE WHAT IS WANTED WITH WHAT ACTUALLY IS IN THE CURRICULUM. THE DIFFERENCE IS THE CURRICULAR NEED.	✓				
B. QUICK ASSESSMENT AND COORDINATION OF THE CURRICULUM—IF AN EXTENSIVE NEEDS ASSESSMENT IS NOT DESIRED, OR AFTER A NEEDS ASSESSMENT IS COMPLETED					✓

(SIMULATED STUDY)

CENTERVILLE READING PROGRAM

STEP I NEEDS ASSESSMENT

(ONE EXAMPLE OF POSSIBLE RESPONSES TO THE CHECKLIST ON PREVIOUS PAGE)

STEP I.　　A.　**IDENTIFY PROBLEM OR NEED**
　　　　1.　IF KNOWN, STATE THE CURRICULUM PROBLEM OR NEED (See page 5 for explanation)

Possible response—Completed:
Students upon entry at the middle school do not seem to read or spell as well as the middle school teachers think they should. The problem is to determine if this is true, and if so, why.

　　　　2.　IF THE NEED IS UNKNOWN OR SHOULD BE VERIFIED, CONDUCT NEEDS ASSESSMENT (See page 5 for explanation)

Possible response—Planning it:
It has never been established what, if any, the specific reading problems are, so a needs assessment is necessary. Mr. King, principal of West Elementary School, will be in charge of the study. Mr. King has asked for a clarification of his role as chairman of this study.

　　　　　　a.　DETERMINE WHAT IS PRESENTLY BEING DONE (WHAT NOW EXISTS), IF ANYTHING (See page 5 for explanation)

Possible response—Planning it:
Teachers in the three elementary schools will list their main content, topics, and reading skills being taught at each grade level. Mr. King will obtain any reading test results that are on file as well as other reading performance records, teacher comments or past curricula evaluations that may help establish what is being accomplished in the present reading program.

　　　　　　b.　DETERMINE WHAT IS WANTED OR INTENDED (See page 6 for explanation)

Possible response—Planning it:
The middle school teachers will make a list of what they want the incoming students to have that they do not have in order to read as they should. The teachers

are to be as specific and detailed as possible with this list.

c.   SELECT OR DEVELOP DATA-GATHERING INSTRUMENT (QUESTION-
     NAIRE, INTERVIEW GUIDE, ETC.) (See page 7 for explanation)

Possible response—Not needed:
No data-gathering instruments other than reading tests that are on file are needed.
The schools all have standardized reading test results on file.

d.   COLLECT AND ORGANIZE INFORMATION (See page 8 for explanation)

Possible response—Planning it:
Mr. King will collect all the main content, topics, etc., listed as being taught by
the elementary teachers, all the reading deficiencies incoming middle students
have according to the middle school teachers, all reading test results, and other
reading performance information available. All this information will be arranged
according to grade levels so it can be studied and analyzed.

e.   ANALYZE DATA: COMPARE WHAT IS WANTED WITH WHAT ACTUALLY
     IS IN THE CURRICULUM. THE DIFFERENCE IS THE CURRICULAR NEED.
     (See page 8 for explanation)

Possible response—Planning it:
A matrix (page 9) will be used to compare what is wanted by the middle school
teachers and what the elementary teachers are doing. Those specific reading topics
listed as needed by the middle school teachers will be listed in the horizontal columns of the matrix and the main topics listed as being covered by the elementary
teachers will be placed in the vertical columns. The reading test results of the
elementary school topics taught will be placed on the matrix if possible. If not,
the results will be put on a separate sheet and attached to the matrix for a quick
reference. Both groups of teachers will crosscheck the topics by placing a check-
mark in the square where the two topics meet if they correspond. If they do not,
the square is left blank. The two groups will then be brought back together to
work out the differences as to the reading topics corresponding or agreeing. Both
Mrs. Doe and Mr. King will be present at this meeting to help reduce disagree-
ments. The squares that are blank, if any, indicate the reading topics which are
not being taught by the elementary reading program that the middle school
teachers think should be. These topics constitute the reading program's need,
which when met will help solve the reading problem. The test results and any
other evaluative data available are used to determine how well reading skills and
topics are being learned by the students, which may also show some needs of the
program.

B. QUICK ASSESSMENT AND COORDINATION OF THE CURRICULUM—IF AN EX-
TENSIVE NEEDS ASSESSMENT IS NOT DESIRED OR AFTER A NEEDS ASSESS-
MENT IS COMPLETED (See page 10 for explanation)

Possible response—Not needed:

Since an extensive needs assessment is going to be conducted, this Substep probably
would not be necessary at this time. However, it as well as other Steps of the ten-step
process could be used to further study the Centerville Reading Program. Some of those
possible studies are described on the next page.

OTHER POSSIBLE STUDIES THAT COULD FOLLOW THE CENTERVILLE READING PROGRAM NEEDS ASSESSMENT USING THE TEN-STEP CURRICULUM PLANNING PROCESS

After determining some of the needs to solve the Centerville Middle School reading problem, it could be decided that the entire reading program should be coordinated. To do this, STEP I (Substep B) of the curriculum planning process, could be used as a guide.

If, in addition to the needs assessment, a look at what other school systems were doing and possible reading innovations in the field of reading was wanted, STEPS VI AND VII would serve as a guide. For a study this extensive, however, STEPS III, IV, AND V probably would be used first to plan and organize for the study.

No doubt, if a study of this magnitude were to be done, goals and objectives of the reading program also would be identified, revised, or developed. To do this, STEP II of the curriculum planning process could be followed.

If very little new or different reading information was found to be needed or wanted, the study could be considered finished with the coordination of the present reading program. (STEP I, Substep B) If, however, a new program, innovation, or a considerable amount of new information is to be incorporated into the present reading program, it will have to be designed or redesigned to fit this school curriculum. The step to be used for curriculum design is STEP VIII of the Ten-Step Curriculum Planning Process. Then, STEP IX, Curriculum Implementation, could be used to guide the implementation of the newly designed reading program. And finally, STEP X, Curriculum Evaluation, could be used to plan the evaluation of the new or redesigned program.

APPENDIX E

(SIMULATED STUDY)

SELECTION OF A SCHOOL COMPUTER EDUCATION PROGRAM USING THE TEN-STEP PROCESS AS A GUIDE

The PTA of your school has money to buy something for the school. Because of the student rage about computer games and all the publicity about computers in education, the PTA is interested in buying computers for your school. The PTA Council has asked the school administration if a computer education program is being planned for the school curricula. If so, what type of computer equipment will be used. The Council would like some guidelines for the types of computers and accessories that could be purchased for the school.

Consider your group to be the administration of this school. Then, using the Ten-Step Curriculum Planning Process, develop a plan to study computer education programs and their use in school curricula to determine if you should start computer classes in your school, and if so, what type of program you will adopt.

Remember, you are not to implement the computer education program, merely decide if you are going to start one, and if so, what type. Also remember, you may not use all of the ten Steps and Sub-steps, at least the first time through; and you may use them in an order other than they are numbered. Do, however, start with Step I and go through them in numerical order first, considering what you will use of each Step, if anything. Check the space on the checklist pages indicating what you intend to do for each Step and Substep. On a separate sheet of paper, describe how you will carry out your plan for the way you checked each one.

ONE EXAMPLE OF POSSIBLE RESPONSES TO THE TEN STEPS FOR DEVELOPING A PLAN TO STUDY COMPUTER EDUCATION PROGRAMS

STEP I.   A.   IDENTIFY PROBLEM OR NEED
1.   IF KNOWN, STATE THE CURRICULUM PROBLEM OR NEED (See page 5 for explanation)

Possible response—Considering it:
The problem is that parents, no doubt at the urging of their youngsters, are asking why the instructors are not teaching about computers and how to use them.

2.   IF THE NEED IS UNKNOWN OR SHOULD BE VERIFIED, CONDUCT NEEDS ASSESSMENT (See page 5 for explanation)

Possible response—Not needed:

The need is not exactly clear. However, the school administration probably does not know enough about computers and how they can be included in the curriculum nor do the parents know enough about them to indicate why they want computers in the school to make a needs assessment beneficial at this time.

STEP II. IDENTIFY, REVISE, OR DEVELOP SCHOOL CURRICULUM/PROGRAM GOALS AND OBJECTIVES (See page 17 for an explanation)

Possible response—Not needed at this stage:

There is not enough known about computers at this point to consider goals and objectives either of the school system or of potential programs. (Planners will probably come back to this Step later.)

STEP III. C. DETERMINE AVAILABILITY OF QUALIFIED PERSONNEL WITHIN THE SCHOOL SYSTEM FOR THE CURRICULUM STUDY (See page 32 for explanation)

Possible response—Planning it:

The school administration would need to consider and select qualified personnel within the system to serve on the study committee. Other parts of this Step would need to be considered after the study committee has been established.

STEP IV. D. STUDY COMMITTEE(S) (AD HOC) (See page 43 for explanation)

Possible response—Planning it:

A study committee should be established to determine the type of computers to be selected and how they could be used in school curricula. Once established, the committee could follow the guidelines in this Step as well as those in Step III to organize for the study of computer education programs.

STEP V. E. STUDY COMMITTEE (AD HOC) CHAIRPERSON (See page 50 for explanation)

Possible response—Planning it:

The chairperson of the study committee could follow guidelines in this Substep for ideas about what to do.

F. TEACHER WHO IS A CURRICULUM COMMITTEE MEMBER (See page 51 for explanation)

Possible response—Planning it:

The chairperson could make the guidelines in this Substep available to the teachers on the committee.

STEP VI. A. IDENTIFY AND LOCATE SEVERAL NEW OR DIFFERENT CURRICULA, PRO-GRAMS, OR INNOVATIONS. GATHER INFORMATION BY: (See page 56 for explanation)

Possible response—Planning it:
This is where the study committee begins their work. The committee could divide into subcommittees and contact the sources suggested in this Step, as well as other available sources, to identify and locate several computer education programs appropriate for school curricula use.

B. ANALYZE NEW CURRICULA OR PROGRAMS BY EXAMINING EACH FOR: (See page 57 for explanation)

Possible response—Planning it:
The study committee could analyze each of the computer education programs identified in part A of this Step in terms of the items listed in this Substep.

STEP VII. A. ASSESS EACH POSSIBLE NEW CURRICULUM OR PROGRAM
1. DESCRIBE HOW IT WILL MEET THE STATED CURRICULAR NEED (See page 61 for explanation)

Possible response—Planning it:
The study committee should describe how each identified computer education program could meet the need stated in Step I. The committee may decide to go back to Step I and restate the need or conduct a needs assessment now that more is known about computer education programs and their use in schools.

2. DESCRIBE HOW IT WILL CONTRIBUTE TO THE GOALS OF THE SCHOOL SYSTEM (See page 61 for explanation)

Possible response—Planning it:
The study committee should compare the goals of each identified computer education program with the goals of the school system. If guidelines for developing goals and objectives are needed, see Step II of this planning process.

3. DESCRIBE HOW IT WILL FIT INTO AND WORK IN THIS PARTICULAR SCHOOL SYSTEM IN TERMS OF: (See page 61 for explanation)

Possible response—Planning it:
The study committee should assess each computer education program as to how it will fit into and work in this school system in terms of the items listed in this Substep.

B. SELECT ONE NEW CURRICULUM OR PROGRAM (See page 62 for explanation)

Possible response—Planning it:

The study committee should select the computer education program which best meets the needs, goals, and fits into this school setting; the committee should also list the reasons why and how it does so. This study would be completed with the study committee's recommendation. The committee would first recommend whether or not a computer education program should be started in the school system; if not, why not; but if so, which one is best suited for this school setting and why.

OTHER STEPS OF THE PLANNING PROCESS THAT COULD BE USED IF THE RECOMMENDED COMPUTER EDUCATION PROGRAM IS ADOPTED

If the decision is made to adopt and implement the recommended computer education program:

STEP II   could be used to develop the computer education program's goals and objectives, if necessary. It could also be used to identify, revise, or develop the district's goal, if necessary.

STEP III   could be used to plan and organize the resources and constraints of implementing the new computer education program.

STEP V   could be used to plan the roles and responsibilities of all who are going to be involved in starting the computer education program in this school curriculum.

STEP VIII   could be used to design or redesign the computer education program.

STEP IX   could be used to implement the computer education program.

STEP X   could be used to evaluate the computer education program.

REFERENCES

GENERAL CURRICULUM PLANNING PROCESSES

(THE CURRICULUM PLANNING PROCESSES AND PROCEDURES IN THESE REFERENCES DEAL WITH MORE THAN ONE OF THE STEPS IN THE TEN-STEP PROCESS; THEREFORE, THEY ARE LISTED AS GENERAL REFERENCES.)

Adams, Don. "Economic Models Planning and Educational Decisions." *Theory Into Practice*, February, 1973, *12*, 59-68.

Alexander, Lawrence T. and Yelon, Stephen L. "The Use of a Common Experiential Referent in Instructional System Design." *Educational Technology*, April, 1969, *9*, 44-46.

Buell, Clayton E. "Guidelines for Curriculum Development." *Educational Leadership*, December, 1968, *26*, 293-297.

Bulach, Cletus R. "An Organizational Plan for Curriculum Development." *Educational Leadership*, January, 1978, *35*, 308-312.

Coger, Rick. "Educational Needs Assessment: A Systematic Approach." *Journal of Allied Health*, Winter, 1977, *6*, 54-60.

English, Fenwick W. *Improving Curriculum Management in the Schools*. Washington, D.C.: Council for Basic Education, 1980.

Georgiades, William. "A Time To do Or Die, Curriculum Change: What Are the Ingredients?" *NASSP Bulletin*, March, 1980, *64*, 70-75.

Gottesman, Alexander M. "Applying a Model in Curriculum Planning." *NASSP Bulletin*, September, 1977, *61*, 24-30.

Grady, Michael P. "Formal Planning is the Key to Effective Program Development." *NASSP Bulletin*, March, 1981, *65*, 44-47.

Hancock, Joseph Ray. "Curriculum Change in English: A Process of Improvement by Cooperative Change." *English Journal*, April, 1974, *63*, 46-48.

Holland, Thomas C.; Grobe, Robert P.; and Denton, William T. "A Scheme for School-Based Change and Decision Making." *NASSP Bulletin*, October, 1977, *61*, 31-41.

Hunkins, Francis P. *Curriculum Development: Program Improvement*. Columbus: Charles E. Merrill,

1980.

Jacobs, James. "A Model for Program Development and Evaluation." *Theory Into Practice*, February, 1974, *13*, 15-21.

Jordan, Lucille G. "Systematizing Curricular Planning and Implementation: What a Supervisor Can Do." *Educational Leadership*, October, 1978, *36*, 41-45.

Karmos, Joseph S. and Jacko, Carol M. "Innovations: A Note of Caution." *NASSP Bulletin*, October, 1977, *61*, 47-56.

Kratz, Robert N. "Educational Planning: If You're Not Ahead, You're Behind." *NASSP Bulletin*, November, 1972, *56*, 26-31.

Mosrie, David. "Assessing School Needs: A Practical Approach." *NASSP Bulletin*, November, 1980, *64*, 64-67.

Niedermeyer, Fred and Yelon, Stephen. "Los Angeles Aligns Instruction with Essential Skills." *Educational Leadership*, May, 1981, *38*, 618-620.

Reed, James and Bakken, John. "The Classroom Teacher and Curriculum Development—A New Approach Suggested." *Man/Society/Technology*, December, 1972, *32*, 147-150.

Stoops, Emery; Rafferty, Max; and Johnson, Russell E. *Handbook of Educational Administration, A Guide for the Practitioner*. Boston: Allyn and Bacon, 1975.

Thompson, Donald L. and Borsari, Leonard R. "An Overview of Management by Objectives for Guidance and Counseling Services." *The School Counselor*, June, 1978, *25*, 172-177.

Thoms, Denis F. "From Needs Assessment to Implementation: A Planning and Action Guide." *Educational Technology*, July, 1978, 5-9.

Toll, Stanley, "A Implementation Strategy for 'Values Clarification'." *The Clearing House*, May, 1977, *50*, 385-389.

Turner, Harold E. "Curriculum Development, Process and People." *Education*, November-December, 1969, *90*, 170-173, 182.

Walker, Decker F. "A Naturalistic Model for Curriculum Development." *School Review*, November, 1971, *80*, 51-65.

Wasserman, Selma. "Teachers as Curriculum-Makers." *Childhood Education*, March, 1976, *51*, 242-247.

Wickert, Jack J. "Criteria for Curriculum Development." *Educational Leadership*, January, 1973, *30*, 339-342.

Williams, William H. "Major Steps in Developing Curriculum." *Industrial Education*, September, 1971, *60*, 79-81.

DATE DUE

DE 25 '03			
MAY 3 1 2011			

GAYLORD   PRINTED IN U.S.A